The Roar of the Crowd

The Roar
of the Crowd

HOW TELEVISION AND PEOPLE POWER
ARE CHANGING THE WORLD

Michael J. O'Neill

TIMES 𝕿 BOOKS

RANDOM HOUSE

All rights reserved under International and Pan-American
Copyright Conventions. Published in the United States by
Times Books, a division of Random House, Inc., New York,
and simultaneously in Canada by Random House of Canada
Limited, Toronto.

Library of Congress Cataloging-in-Publication Data

O'Neill, Michael J., 1922 –
The roar of the crowd: how television and people power are
changing the world / Michael J. O'Neill.
    p.   cm.
Includes bibliographical references and index.
ISBN 0-8129-2078-3
1. Mass media — Political aspects. 2. Democracy. I. Title.
P95.8.O54 1993
302.23 — dc20   92-56836

BOOK DESIGN BY REBECCA AIDLIN

Manufactured in the United States of America
9   8   7   6   5   4   3   2
First Edition

Contents

Acknowledgments

LIKE THE FEDERAL GOVERNMENT, I am deeply in debt to many people, for all the facts, ideas, criticism, and support they contributed to this imperfect enterprise. I am especially grateful to Joseph E. Slater, distinguished diplomat and former president of the Aspen Institute, for his original enthusiasm for the project and his sustained personal encouragement, and to Lloyd N. Morrisett and the John & Mary R. Markle Foundation for their generous financial support.

I also benefited over the years from many lively exchanges with Walter Wriston, a seminal thinker and innovator who has been light-years ahead of most other business leaders in recognizing the economic and political implications of the global communications revolution.

I drew on the work of many scholars but I am especially grateful to Ellen Mickiewicz, S. Frederick Starr, and Eileen Mahoney, who provided many insights and suggestions that helped to reduce, if not eliminate, errors of thought and fact.

My editors, Steve Wasserman and Ken Gellman, ordered painful cuts and organizational reforms that greatly improved the clarity of the final draft. Elisabeth Malkin, my principal research assistant, worked zestfully in the same cause, peppering me with constructive criticisms as well as facts. For briefer periods, Michael Vachon and Jack Metcalfe also provided very valuable advice as well as research help.

Susan M. S. Brown edited the manuscript with a marvelous ear for language and eye for factual detail and argument. But over the months of gestation and writing, my most constant copyreader and sharpest critic was my wife, Mary Jane. Now an executive but formerly a reporter and editor, she slogged through several drafts and never ceased to discover flaws I had missed.

Finally, this book never could have happened if it had not been for many other people in Russia, Eastern Europe, China, and other countries who willingly shared their experiences while their own lives and careers were being convulsed by revolutionary change. Government officials, university professors, newspaper editors, television anchors, and innumerable ordinary citizens gave freely of their time even when they really had no time. It was amazing, and I am grateful.

The Roar of the Crowd

I

Contagion of Freedom

IT SEEMED SO SMALL, SO PITIFULLY small to carry such a burden of history. The little shrine was huddled in front of a low wall on the overpass in Moscow where Kalinin Avenue crosses Tchaikovsky Street. A display of chrysanthemums and lilies, festooned with red and white ribbons, stood in the background. Other flowers, a few in pots but most lying loose on the ground, were gathered around the framed photograph of a young man. To the right were a Russian Orthodox icon and two tapers flickering faintly in a morning drizzle. Cars sped by on Kalinin's broad six lanes, unwatching. Only four women stood gazing at the photograph. There was no inscription, but they knew the name: Vladimir Usov. He had been crushed under the treads of a tank during a night of confusion and fear only three weeks earlier, one of three youths to die during a brief, impulsive, and personal defense of liberty in a nation that had seen no real liberty in a thousand years.

The shrine recalled only an incident, a fleeting instant, a mere mote in the heavens of time, and yet, as caprice would decide, it also commemorated a great turning point in human experience. During an incredible seventy-two hours in August 1991, the whole empire of totalitarian communism—seventy-four years of repression, terror, false utopian claims, and worldwide aggression against Western liberalism—came crashing down. Whether democracy would rise from the ruins was an unsettled question, but when the Kremlin hard-liners, the bumbling Gang of Eight, failed to overthrow Mikhail Gorbachev, the Russian people were suddenly freer than they had ever been before, even including those few frantic years of parliamentary testing before World War I. "For the first time in their history," said George F. Kennan, "they have turned their back on the manner in which they've been ruled, not just in the Soviet period but in the centuries before. They have demanded a voice in designing their own society. Even 1917 had nothing quite like this."[1] The fall of the capital of communism climaxed the great liberating revolutions that swept through Eastern Europe in 1989 and spread to the Baltics and to the Soviet Union's own restive republics. For the world, no less than for Russia, August 1991 marked the end of one age and the beginning of another.

The Kremlin coup was one of those defining acts that suddenly connect millions of people to a single moment in time. Lives running in different directions, self-concerned and untouching, were suddenly joined in one incandescent instant of shared emotion. In 1917 it took four to six weeks for Russian villages to get word of Czar Nicholas's abdication. But news of the coup traveled with electronic speed through eleven time zones to reach across the world's largest nation in a matter of minutes. From Moscow and Leningrad to Tbilisi and the Kamchatka peninsula, people quickly learned that something momentous was taking place. They would recall later exactly where they were when they heard the news. They would remember what they were doing, what they were thinking, how frightened, calm, or indifferent they were. For many, the coup would become a new

4

border in time, a new line drawn through their lives marking a "before" and an "after," a line from which to measure the present and the future.

For Mikhail N. Poltoranin the line was drawn at seven o'clock in the morning of August 19, when there was a loud knock on the door of his dacha near Arkhangelskoye, an aristocratic country retreat preserved for communist gentry on the Moscow River, sixteen miles west of the Kremlin. Russia's genial minister of mass information was having breakfast with his wife before going into the woods on a mushroom hunt. So he was irritated when he was confronted at the door by the chief of Boris Yeltsin's bodyguards, who said the Russian president wanted to see him immediately. "I'm sick of always being interrupted by some crisis," Poltoranin complained. "I'm going off to collect mushrooms." But the bodyguard insisted. He had to go immediately to Yeltsin's dacha 200 yards away; it was urgent. Indeed it was. A state of emergency had been proclaimed, and, more immediately alarming, Lt. Gen. Pavel S. Grachev had called with a warning that he had been ordered to arrest Yeltsin. The general urged the president to leave quickly because he could not stall long before sending paratroopers to the dacha.

Poltoranin and other close aides, including the Russian secretary of state, Gennady Burbulis, and Parliamentary Chairman Ruslan Kahasbulatov, hastily drafted a statement condemning the coup and calling for resistance. They broke into a nearby staff office to make photocopies and then, armed with machine guns and pistols, raced back to Moscow with Yeltsin. "Daddy," Yeltsin's daughter told him as he put on a bulletproof vest, "now, everything depends on you."[2] Poltoranin hid copies of the manifesto under a carpet and gave his driver a secret address where they should be delivered in case the official party was captured. In one of many ironies, the military convoy en route to Yeltsin's dacha and the little band of rebellion passed within yards of each other as they sped in opposite directions along the Ring Road. But the armored personnel carriers never stopped, and Yeltsin made it safely to Russia's white marble parliament building. From there he would raise a public storm that would rescue his old antagonist Mikhail Gorbachev, destroy his enemies in the Kremlin, set Great Russia onto an uncertain new course, and break open international relationships that had been locked in the Cold War for forty-six years.

Yeltsin's success was made of many things—his own decisive leadership, the liberating effects of Gorbachev's perestroika, economic failure, a bankrupt political system, bumbling party hacks, and, inspiringly, young people raised on glasnost, untrained in fear, and zestfully eager to exercise freedoms their parents never had in order to create a new society their parents never imagined. But utterly decisive during the hours of danger and decision was something else: communications—slow years of public awakening, then glasnost, and finally the nearly instantaneous merging of people and technology in a climactic swirl of mobilized opinion, street action, and counterrevolution.

It was a spontaneous combustion of couriers, telephones, faxes, newspapers, radio, television, videotapes, computers, and satellites that relayed Yeltsin's defiance around the earth. Gorbachev, who in captivity depended on the BBC, Radio Liberty, and Voice of America for news of his own fate, conceded later that the independent media he had derided so often was "a wall preventing dictatorship" during the coup.[3] But Yeltsin knew this instinctively. From the beginning, he realized that to defeat the plotters he had to establish a lifeline of messages, appeals, and defiant visual gestures, that he had to be connected quickly to the Russian people, to hesitant generals and sympathetic young soldiers, and to Western leaders.

So it was at 9:00 A.M. that he and his lieutenants issued the *ukaz* or proclamation they had drafted in Arkhangelskoye. Addressed "To the Citizens of Russia," it denounced the Kremlin takeover as "a reactionary, unconstitutional coup d'état" and urged massive popular resistance. By 10:00 A.M. telephones, copiers, and faxes were working furiously in the Russian White House, in Moscow City Hall, and, increasingly with every hour, in offices and factories in many parts of the city. Despite fumbling KGB attacks on communications lines, and radio, TV, and newspaper blackouts, the rallying cry went out across Russia in a thousand unofficial ways, from pamphlets plastered on subway walls and clandestine radio and newspaper reports to electronic mail and foreign television broadcasts.

As tanks ringed the White House and young defenders built barricades to block their way, journalists at *Moscow News, Nezavisimaya Gazeta,* and other banned newspapers scrambled to word processors, copiers, and even out-of-town presses to produce quickie news reports that volunteers distributed around Moscow. Famous TV anchors like Alexander Lyubimov and Vladimir Molchanov dispatched camera crews to cover the White House and other action scenes, sending tapes to cities like Leningrad where TV stations were still running free from Kremlin control. The Cable News Network and other foreign networks were meanwhile beaming a steady stream of news and pictures to Soviet *Sputnik* satellites that the KGB never touched, and some of the coverage flowed back into the Soviet Union. Reports from CNN, a standard prop in government ministries and even in some Moscow apartments, quickly reached the key players in the unfolding drama, signaling Yeltsin, for example, that President Bush had been distressingly equivocal in his first public reaction to the coup. "Praise be information technology! Praise be CNN," said Eduard A. Shevardnadze. "Anyone who owned a parabolic antenna able to see this network's transmissions had a complete picture of what was happening."[4]

Without intending to be helpful, the state television system, Gosteleradio, made its own surprising contribution to the democratic cause. After announcing the national emergency on that first Monday morning, Channel One played the signature music the Kremlin reserves for grave occasions like the death of Stalin or the removal of a general secretary. So while tanks were rumbling through Moscow's streets, millions of viewers were swathed in the gentle melodies of *Swan Lake* and Chopin. "Then I really got scared," said a woman in Leningrad, Alla Yulievna. "Here Chopin is not music, it's a diagnosis. They always play it to calm us down."[5] In keeping with custom, announcers broke in from time to time with official pronouncements but did not find it newsworthy that crowds were barricading the White House and chanting "Daloy Huntu! Yeltsin! Yeltsin!"— "Down with the junta!" It was as if the freedom forces did not exist. But later on Monday something incredible happened: the national evening news show *Vremya*, which had a policy of ignoring Yeltsin, suddenly filled the screen with him. There he was in the now famous scene outside the White House, standing on top of a T-72 army tank, surrounded at the time by no more than 200 supporters, reading his denunciation of the coup.

The conspirators thought the coverage would prove their claim that Moscow was torn by mob violence and that this would win public support for a military crackdown to restore order. Instead, those unforgettable pictures created an indelible symbol of personal bravery and political defiance. They made Yeltsin a larger-than-life hero, an instant legend, like the unknown youth who stood in front of the tank in Tiananmen Square in 1989. Thousands of young Russians in Moscow and Leningrad rallied to their president's call. The coup leaders were further ravaged by indecision about the use of force. And in other countries the image of a strong anticoup movement was burned into the consciousness of millions, including President Bush. As the scenes flooded in from Moscow, he was deeply affected by Yeltsin's display of courage. He became convinced there was solid opposition to the Gang of Eight and finally threw his full support behind the Russian leader he and his aides had previously snubbed.

In addition to making a hero out of their chief antagonist, the bumbling conspirators committed the fatal error of putting themselves on national television. In contrast to Yeltsin's tank-top dynamism, they exposed the vast Soviet audience to a dismal mural of five gray suits, mug-shot faces, and witless personalities. Gennady Yanayev, acting Soviet president and spokesman for the ensemble, was so nervously uncertain during the staged news conference that his hands shook as if they were palsied. He seemed as unnerved by planted cotton candy questions as he was by a few unplanned inquiries from independent reporters, including a barbed suggestion that the emergency committee had used ex-Chilean strongman Augusto Pinochet as a model for their power grab. Television, with its X-ray examination of character, turned Yanayev and his fellow committeemen into blobs of incompetence who gave the impression they could not win a rigged election much less lead a nation. They were visually discredited like other party hacks who had been voted into oblivion after television coverage of parliamentary meetings exposed their stupidity to local constituents. As the writer Tatyana Tolstaya observed, it should have been obvious the takeover would fail "the moment that we saw the faces of the plotters and the trembling hands of Gennady Yanayev, and heard the incoherent stammering speeches."[6]

During the early hours of the coup, when the first priority was to get the word of Yeltsin's resistance to the people in Moscow and elsewhere in the sprawling Russian Republic, a communications bucket brigade sprang into existence with amazing speed. Most surprising was an independent computer network called Relcom that links Moscow to more than 500 centers in eighty other Soviet cities and can be plugged directly into the United States and Europe through international e-mail systems like Euronet and Internet. Yeltsin and his high command were not even aware of the network, but one of its founders, Vadim G. Antonov, swung into action as soon as he heard the first coup bulletins on CNN. A brilliant young mathematician and UNIX operating system expert, Antonov heads a computer cooperative called Demos. He and nearly two dozen colleagues immediately began feeding Yeltsin's decrees, Interfax news dispatches, and anticoup advisories onto their high-speed system. They also passed on to the Russian White House printouts of news and messages pouring in from the United States. "I hope we'll be able to communicate during the first days," said Antonov in an early message. "Communists cannot rape Mother Russia once again!" At a more frantic period, he filed a complaint about a glut of incoming traffic: "Please stop flooding the only narrow channel. . . . We need the bandwidth to help organize the resistance. Please do not—even unintentionally—help these fascists!" Danger was another problem, especially outside Moscow, where some centers were being threatened by local hard-liners. "Don't worry," said one message. "We're okay, though frightened and angry!"

An odd twist was that the most reliable communications

between Yeltsin and his chief ally, Leningrad Mayor Anatoly A. Sobchak, turned out to be the Soviet government's internal telephone network. It was far superior to the notoriously flaky public system because it operated in digital codes. The Leningrad City Council had been using this and a Demos computer to communicate with Western businesses. During the coup, the system was employed to provide a direct computer-to-computer connection from the Leningrad council to the Moscow council, which, like the White House, was a center of anticoup activity. Another more bizarre fact is that one of the Gang of Eight was indirectly responsible for the excellent communications between Yeltsin's headquarters and a shadow government headquarters he had established in Sverdlovsk as a fallback in case his White House was overrun. In that Ural Mountain redoubt, the computer center handling the rush of reports from the White House had actually been set up by a subsidiary of a company of which Alexander I. Tizyakov was a director. Tizyakov was the military-industrial member of the Kremlin plot; he could take pride in the center's splendid contribution to the failure of his own conspiracy.

Major radio and TV outlets in Moscow were effectively blacked out or forced to operate under rigid Kremlin direction. But one rebellious ten-kilowatt radio station kept popping on and off the air while playing hide-and-seek with the KGB. *Moscow Echo,* a protégé of the Moscow City Council which broadcasts from a tiny studio only a shout from Red Square, was invaded on the morning of the coup by a squad of KGB plainclothesmen. The officer in charge announced that, although he personally was an *Echo* fan, he had orders to shut the station down. He was persuaded, however, that he need not close the studio; he could do his duty by merely disconnecting a cable. This knocked the station off the air but left the staff in command of all the telephones, recording equipment, and studio facilities they needed to cover the coup story.

The first night they recorded a ten-minute news report which the BBC and Radio Liberty then broadcast back into the Soviet Union. On the following day a Yeltsin sympathizer in the government secretly reconnected the cable, and *Moscow Echo* burst forth with a full round of live broadcasts from inside and outside the White House. In one of these, Russian Vice President Alexander V. Rutskoi sounded the alarm that troops were preparing to attack Tuesday night. The broadcasting flurry alerted the KGB, and they cut the cable again. This time, the combative *Echo* editors employed another ruse: they used ordinary telephones to relay news reports and recordings of Yeltsin officials directly to the radio transmitter some miles away, and, despite orders to the contrary, technicians put these on the air. Once again, *Moscow Echo* was going full throttle. The KGB eventually caught up with the new deception and switched off the transmitter. "But by this time," said Sergey Fonton, *Echo*'s deputy editor, "the takeover was already failing, and we were back on the air full-time on August 22."

Moscow Echo was not the only free radio struggling to be heard; Yeltsin's team established their own *Radio Russia* inside the parliament building.[7] Contrary to many news reports, the Russian defenses were not as impromptu as they seemed. A coup and some kind of attack had been expected for months. In December, Eduard Shevardnadze had quit as foreign minister with the warning that antireformers were plotting a dictatorship. The hard-liners showed their muscle in January, when they sent OMON or "black beret" troops into Lithuania and Latvia in a bloody assault against independence movements. And they followed this with a dry-run takeover in June, when Prime Minister Valentin S. Pavlov, with the support of the KGB and fellow right-wing ministers, demanded that Gorbachev surrender all his emergency powers to him. Reading the signs, Yeltsin and his colleagues expected the worst and began making preparations that included creating secret caches of guns, gas masks, medical supplies, and—with an especially high priority—radio and TV equipment.

So it was that as the coup began in August, a Russian team drove to a secret rendezvous, loaded transmitters into a blue armored car, and headed for the White House. As they moved through Moscow's streets, they worried that they might be intercepted. But military patrols, assuming the car carried a routine shipment of money, only waved them on with friendly salutes, and the transmitters were safely installed in an improvised basement studio. Although officials managed to make only two TV transmissions, they kept their radio station going around the clock with appeals, warnings, personal statements by Yeltsin and his lieutenants, and news reports delivered by Lyubimov, Molchanov, and other celebrities. *Radio Russia* was no match for the powerful Central TV or even for *Moscow Echo.* It was more effective than its low power suggested, however, because it was able to transmit on AM as well as by shortwave under two different call signs, R3A and R3B. And the public was alerted to the special frequencies by the free-ranging media.

Leading the media forces were militantly independent journalists like Vitali Tretiakov, founding editor of *Nezavisimaya Gazeta,* and Yegor Yakovlev, editor of *Moscow News,* who was later picked by Yeltsin to be the new head of Gosteleradio. When the coup exploded on August 19 and Yeltsin proclaimed his opposition, *Gazeta* staffers swarmed over the story, despite charges they were acting illegally. By evening they were ready to go to press with a regular edition when they were cut off from their *Izvestia* printing plant by the KGB. Working through the night, they produced a two-page packet of news and comment and faxed it to other newspapers, news agencies, and foreign news bureaus and embassies. One headline: "We Shall Live Until the Day We Are Free." Volunteers operating copiers and desktop printers in scores of offices, including the new Moscow Commodities Exchange and the Soros Foundation, made thousands of copies for circulation all over the city. Even more surprising, the *Gazeta* transmitted a full-size paper to Paris, where it was printed in French and widely distributed with a six-column headline proclaiming Tretiakov's appeal "to the free journalists of the entire world" to help save his country's "free press . . . and nascent democracy."[8]

The next morning, August 21, *Nezavisimaya Gazeta* published a four-page, photocomposed edition with extensive news reports and some biting comment: "Now everyone can see Pugo, Yazov, Kryuchkov and the rest of them for what they really are. Now everyone realizes there is no room for hesitation and vacillation." On the same day, *Moscow News* produced eight pages of galleys with headlines like "Before It's Too Late!" referring to the illegality of the coup and the ruin it threatened, and "Russian Power at Work," describing the democratic resistance. In addition, the *News* and the *Gazeta* pooled their talents with nine other independent newspapers to publish a full-size free paper. This was called *Obshchaya Gazeta* or "Common Paper," and it led with the headline "Democracy Must Know How to Defend Itself." Poltoranin, Russia's information minister and one of the project's organizers, immediately issued a publishing license so that the coup leaders could not say the paper was illegal.

The new journalists of the Soviet Union, young offspring of glasnost, aggressive, resourceful, protective of their own special freedoms but also infected with the promise of democracy, fought spontaneously to keep the channels of information open to the public. Even some of those held under lock and key in state-controlled newspapers and television centers inflicted wounds on the hard-liners with small acts of sabotage. In one case, a Yeltsin statement was slipped into a Central TV script by staffers from the suppressed TSN television news program. In another, more daring move, Gosteleradio technicians drove a communications truck up to the White House to help CNN's Bruce Connover set up a video microwave relay. "Young journalists were the driving force of the counterrevolution," said the political analyst Alexei Izyumov, formerly of the Soviet Academy of Sciences. "They behaved very bravely in helping to mobilize public support in the two key cities, Moscow and Leningrad." Shevardnadze, himself a prominent figure in the anticoup struggle, was even more expansive. "With its spiritedness and courage, its inventiveness, and its contempt for the conspirators," he said, "this independent journalism illustrated the triumph of ideas long suppressed by the system: freedom of information is an inalienable aspect of freedom and democracy."[9]

The role of the media was critical because, like the tree falling in an empty forest, Yeltsin's resistance did not exist until it was seen and heard. It became real only when it became news and when millions of people were connected to the White House by the shared knowledge of move and countermove in an epochal encounter. The crowds that took to the streets were only a small fraction of the general population, seeming to confirm the proverbial apathy of the Russian masses. Yet small as they were, the demonstrations reflected deep social changes that in the final analysis were crucial to the outcome: changes such as the rise of a new generation of independent, pro-freedom young people in the army as well as in civil life, the decline of personal fear as a coercing fact of daily political experience, and overwhelming popular repudiation of the Communist Party.

Quickie polls during the August crisis showed that only half those questioned considered the Emergency Committee unlawful. But no one—not even party apparatchiks—staged any demonstrations to cheer it on. Nor did the public show the slightest regret or even interest, as Leonid Gordon wrote in the *Moscow News,* when the party and all the "birthmarks of socialism" were swept away in the coup's aftermath.[10] Despite many contradictory currents in Russian public opinion, there was much wider support for democratic reform, especially among the younger generation, than was suggested by Yeltsin's thin ranks of defenders.

News and communications during the coup had a number of effects. Rapid circulation of Yeltsin's call for help sent thousands of people through Manezh Square and on to the White House to raise barricades against tanks. Telephones, radios, newspapers, and, to a limited degree, television sets also carried the summons of resistance to the rest of Russia and the other republics. In a matter of a few hours, government officials, democratic leaders, journalists, miners, and factory workers were busy communicating over a giant electronic latticework. Groups, fearful of acting alone, were encouraged to take a stand when they saw or heard that 300,000 people were rallying in Leningrad or that coal miners were striking in the Kuzbass and Donbass regions.

The mutineers were conversely shaken by the same news as it appeared on CNN and rolled in from independent news services like Interfax. Interfax's founder, Mikhail V. Komissar, said the Kremlin was anxiously calling every few minutes for news updates that only certified the growing democratic opposition. All the reports, circulating rapidly through many layers of society and of political power, set off their own secondary reactions. One was that many fence sitters were nudged over to Yeltsin's side, and this, in turn, intensified a public impression that the plot was failing. Another reaction was that extensive reporting about young soldiers and officers being unwilling to attack civilians made the coup leaders increasingly doubtful about their ability to use military force. Television showed youths at the White House barricades saying they were "ready to die" while tank crews assured questioners they would never shoot.

In a different way, communications also played an important role in the drama that unfolded in the presidential vacation compound at Cape Foros on the Black Sea. Mikhail and Raisa Gorbachev had been swimming and playing with their daughter, Irina, her husband, Anatoly Wergansky, and their grandchildren, Anastasia and Oksana. It had been a pleasant time, but on Sunday evening, August 18, two actions were noted in the KGB log at the Moscow headquarters of the Soviet government's special communications network:

> 17:55—Comrade A. G. Beda orders the communications lines linking Yalta and Foros with Kiev, Simferopol, and Sevastopol switched over to manual operation mode.
> 20:00—All the above-said lines have been switched to manual operation mode.[11]

The words were supremely innocuous, intentionally so, but they marked the beginning of a personal and political nightmare. With the switch to manual operation, all of Gorbachev's telephone connections were cut off, "including the satellite line."[12] When a Kremlin delegation demanded, and failed to get, his resignation, he was held captive at his dacha, Zarya, surrounded by KGB guards and denied all contact with the outside world.

During the tense first days, Gorbachev was bolstered in his defiance by news of Russian resistance that he got not from the propaganda on Gosteleradio but from foreign broadcasts the communists formerly had jammed. And in another marvelous bow to media technology, he secretly recorded his own repudiation of the coup with a small video camera the family had been using to tape Anastasia practicing her ballet lessons. As a result, the now historic video of the presidential manifesto still shows brief glimpses of Gorbachev's granddaughter in a leotard doing her pliés and élevés.

On the larger scale of international relations, the crisis in Moscow demonstrated—better perhaps than anything else in recent times—the extraordinary power of global communications to affect decisions and outcomes. George Bush, a *Guinness Book* telephoner, jumped on the line to world leaders beginning at 5:00 on the first morning of the coup. At 7:45 A.M. he gave reporters his first cautiously equivocal reaction, and the news flashed by satellite to Moscow. A disappointed Yeltsin thought it was urgent to persuade Bush to take a stronger stand; he badly needed this to undermine support for the Emergency Committee in the Soviet military and with the general public. An urgent Yeltsin message, citing popular resistance to the coup and the reactionary threat to democracy, sped over a secure satellite circuit from the U.S. Embassy to the State Department and then to *Air Force One*, which was en route to Washington from Bush's vacation home in Kennebunkport, Maine.

After arriving in Washington, Bush quickly put more firepower into his position. Impressed by Yeltsin's courage and adopting some of the language in Yeltsin's message, the president issued a statement denouncing the coup as "unconstitutional" and fully backing the Russian leader. And on the following day, Bush voiced his support in trademark telephone calls to the man he had come to see as a "very courageous individual . . . standing firm for democracy."[13]

The calls had to be patched through a standard AT&T circuit because the special government telephone in Yeltsin's office had been cut off. The tug-of-war between the KGB and Yeltsin, Gorbachev, Bush, and other Western leaders was revealed with inanimate terseness in secret logs. Excerpts:

August 19

15:14—Comrade Beda [KGB] orders special lines to Yeltsin cut off.

15:25—The lines have been cut off.

22:02—A call placed from Washington. US President Bush wants to speak to Gorbachev. Comrade Volkov has been informed.

22:17—Comrade Volkov [KGB] suggests that Bush speak to the acting President, Comrade Yanayev.

22:21—The American side rejects the suggestion. They want to speak to Gorbachev and no one else. This was reported to Comrade Volkov.

August 20

13:42—A trunk call was placed from Washington. Bush wants to speak to Comrade Yeltsin. Comrade Volkov is informed.

14:07—Comrade Volkov forbids the connection.

14:17—Washington has been repeatedly explained that Yeltsin is not available since his telephone can't be located.

16:55—Another call for Yeltsin. This was reported to Comrade Volkov.

13:44—French President Mitterrand wants to speak to Comrade Gorbachev. This was reported to Comrade Volkov.

14:07—Comrade Volkov suggests to Mitterrand that

the latter be put through to Comrade Yanayev instead.[14]

Although tanks, armored cars, and troops were sent into Moscow in the time-honored ritual of coups d'état, it was communications that proved to be the final arbiter between victory and defeat. While the plotters obviously could have imposed more controls than they did, it was clear that the old police-state tools no longer worked. The electronic age had penetrated too far into the Soviet Union; virtually nothing could prevent the countercoup news from escaping. As it was, television images—the shadowy night views of young Muscovites manning barricades and attacking tanks on the approaches to the White House—delivered the message of resistance as nothing else could. In the tight focus of TV cameras, 30,000 demonstrators stood for a nation. Pictures, more than words or even telephone calls, fast-charged emotions in the free world and moved key leaders like Britain's John Major and President Bush to back Yeltsin publicly. These endorsements, beamed instantly to the Soviet Union, were then used by Yeltsin to convince public opinion that the West was on his side and, most important, that he probably would win. "I'm sure that if they had not seen the Russian leadership putting up a resistance," said Yeltsin's longtime close aide Pavel Voschanov, "then these world leaders would have continued to be cautious."[15]

All the international maneuvering that put the United States and other Western powers into play—the high-speed planning, decisions, and actions—also operated in a new world of electronic diplomacy. The U.S. Embassy in Moscow, which did not even have CNN, was little more than an occasional message center. The president and his top advisers were operating on facts they got from CNN and other media rather than reports from diplomats trailing far behind events. Bush, of course, worked the phones to consult personally with more than a dozen foreign leaders. And when he took action, he did so on television rather than through diplomatic channels. As one official put it, the first thought was not how to cable instructions to American diplomats but how to get a statement on CNN that would shape an allied response. "Diplomatic communications just can't keep up with CNN," he said.[16]

In many ways, the August Revolution was a singular event with its own Russian character, resonant of old cycles of reform and repression from Alexander II through the Zemstvo Congress and Khrushchev thaw to Gorbachev's perestroika. But the tiny shrine on the Kalinin Avenue overpass was not unique. Other candles had been burning in other cities: in Bucharest and Timisoara, Prague, East Berlin, Dresden and Leipzig, Vilnius and Riga, Tirana and Sofia, Rangoon and Beijing, where decrees could not banish memories of bloodshed in Tiananmen Square. In fact, the upheaval in the Soviet Union was not an exception but a part—a dramatic but integral part—of a vast process of global change. Nations are everywhere in tumultuous transition: waves of nationalism sweeping over the ruins of collapsing regimes and empires. Failure erasing the utopian dreams of communism. Western domination receding before the rising tides of Asia. Popular movements challenging the power of ruling elites, toppling authoritarian leaders from Central Europe to the Philippines and South Korea, and frightening revolutionary relics in Beijing and Pyongyang. Whole civilizations rearranging themselves into a new interdependent and multipolar world, which even the daring could not foresee only a decade ago.

Sensations flash through our lives at electronic speeds, compressing time. The work of ages is completed in a century, then in a lifetime or a generation or even a decade. The

Cold War disappears in less than three years. Everything is in motion; patterns of national and international life break up and re-form like ice floes in the spring. Many trends converge from different directions. But a central energizing force in all that is happening is the communications revolution.

An astonishing surge in new communications technology has for the first time in history put nearly all the earth's peoples in continuous, emotional contact with one another. Radio, television, computers, and satellites flood the world with images and information, expanding the universe of daily experience, accelerating the tempos of life to nervous limits, and compressing nations into ever closer, more dependent, and tenser relationships. Communications are the carriers of revolution, not only in visible finales like the Moscow coup but also, more important, in the deeper, earlier stages, when infusions of new knowledge and human contacts profoundly alter social and economic trends and pave the road to political upheaval. The increasing penetration of Western ideas into Soviet life over many years, but notably since the beginning of glasnost in 1985, was one of the transforming factors that led ultimately to the popular rejection and then collapse of the Communist Party. Yeltsin's victory was not so much a revolution as the certification of a revolution already in progress.

It is the argument of this book that there is, in fact, a strong link between the global expansion of modern communications and the enormous events that have been traveling like a storm front across the end of the twentieth century. From the rise of people power and the contagion of freedom in Eastern Europe to the forging of a world economy and the breakdown of political systems in the face of violent change, no other single factor has been more important than the mass transmission of images and information. At least six phenomena are involved:

THE NEW ANATOMY OF KNOWLEDGE

Rapidly advancing technology has extended the range of public knowledge across the barriers of space, illiteracy, and national sovereignty to reach virtually all of the inhabited earth. The sheer volume of information now crashing down upon the human mind is staggering. Equally significant, much of the information is being delivered in an oral-visual form that breaks the monopoly of the world's literate classes. Thanks to television, the daily experiences of mankind are brought down from the skies to city and village alike, to peasant as well as mandarin, and with an emotional intensity words cannot match. The eyes of countless millions are opened to an outside world they have never seen, and their emotional responses are merged by rapid communication into networks of collective opinion. Expanding knowledge and shared responses are bound together in ever widening rings of informed and active publics. The great lost masses of history, the peasants who stood for centuries outside the gates of civic life, are now finding their way inside. "I contend that behind contemporary political turmoil," says the historian William H. McNeill, "the most fundamental change we are witnessing is the politicization of the world's peasantries." Thanks in part to new communications, he says, "peasant populations are ready, as never before, to claim the rights of full citizenship and equality of circumstances with privileged urban dwellers."[17]

THE GLOBAL SPREAD OF MASS SOCIETIES

Mass societies, dense and highly interactive human conglomerates made possible by mass media, are spreading rapidly from the advanced industrial nations to other countries around the world. Communications technology always influences human organization. A society based on the automobile is quite different from one based on travel by foot; the progression from nomadic tribes to crowded cities can be measured in the strata of invention. As the speed of communication rises, social distance shrinks and ever larger numbers of people, widely separated by space, are drawn into common experiences. Human interactions increase exponentially in a whirl of mass media, mass marketing, mass consumerism, and mass culture. Lives once confined to a village become entwined in the affairs of a region or nation. With satellites circling the earth, whole civilizations are intermingled in a new global economy and now stand, in Daniel Bell's words, "on the threshold" of a world society.[18] A place where we already see individual concerns about environmental dangers and human rights becoming national concerns and, increasingly, global political issues.

THE RISE OF PEOPLE POWER

From youths manning the barricades in Moscow to prodemocracy students being massacred in Burma, popular movements have become the daily news of our time. Everywhere people are demanding to be heard, demanding more control over their lives. Many reasons have been cited: economic dissatisfactions, ethnic conflicts, and political rivalries. But a common denominator is the intensification of human interactions, the more acute awareness of similarities as well as differences that modern communications promotes. More fully informed about neighbors near and far, people expand their horizons of interest so that the nature of public affairs is changing. Popular opinion intrudes into the chambers of presidents and kings. "Virtually from the beginning of the Gorbachev leadership," says the Emory University scholar Ellen Mickiewicz, public opinion began playing a more important role largely because of "the dramatic spread of television in the Soviet Union and the enormous public it has attracted."[19]

Even when there are no demonstrators on the streets, collective feelings are formed, polled, and publicized by the mass media so that public opinion is a constantly felt political presence. Nothing says that democracy has to follow popular revolts, as Jacobin France proved long ago or as ethnic clashes and violent nationalism suggest today. But the collaboration of mass information and public opinion is a liberating force that is already restricting the licenses of rulers, so that, for example, military assaults against peaceful protesters were the exception rather than the practice during the climactic events in Eastern Europe. Popular movements are not the same as popular government, but they tend to promote pluralism as against totalitarianism, and they could be signaling a historic event to come: the extension of popular sovereignty to areas of the world never touched before by democracy.

CENTRAL CASTING FOR LEADERS

The surge of people power, the swirling torrents of instant images, the incessant demands for performance rather than thought, and the loss of authority in a sea of fragmenting political power have profoundly and forever changed the definition of political leadership in the information age. Presidents and prime ministers, congressmen and MPs— even strongmen—have all been driven out of their old warrens of private deliberation and self-claimed wisdom. They are now forced to act on the public stage, in front of ever-present cameras, reacting instantly to every public whim, searching constantly for just the right image or just the right sound bite they need to entertain or appease their audiences. Political parties no longer count for much in picking candidates; central casting is the major new recruitment center. Telegenicity—a personality with strong visual and emotional appeal—is more important than the ability to govern a great nation. And even in the accidental circumstance when a leader has both ability and personality, he still must be squeezed into television's mold because that is now the instrument by which he must rule in a world of instantly informed and active publics.

CRISIS OF GOVERNANCE

The electronic revolution is changing the way nations are governed, profoundly altering the balance of power between citizens and governors, magnifying public demands and conflicts, and increasing the velocity of action and reaction beyond the limits of thought. Because the nurturing of public opinion is essential to governing, television is essential to governors. Leaders are defined more by TV images than by knowledge and experience. Media politics becomes a necessity. Rising expectations, fired by TV visions of a better life and promoted by market economies, which are now in such vogue, demand more than governments can deliver. Institutions designed for another age break down; replacements emerge too slowly—if they emerge at all—and political disorder follows. This is immediately evident in a freedom-recovery area like Central Europe, but there is disarray, too, in mature democracies such as the United States. Social, economic, and technological changes are racing so far ahead of political responses that a crisis of governance is as much a general world condition as the special problems of individual nations.

NEW WORLD DISORDER

The whole international system—the tempo of change, the volume of transactions, the nature of relations between nations—has been turned on its head by the onrush of new communications technology. News, data, money, and trade flash along electronic or photonic circuits that ignore borders. Multinational corporations, operating over high-speed networks, bypass outmoded government regulations to create an interdependent global economy. The walls of national sovereignty are chipped away. The affairs of nations are more tightly interwoven; the lines between domestic and foreign policy become blurred. Incredibly, statesmen like Jimmy Carter are called in to certify a foreign country's elections. Workers in one country are more directly affected by workers in another. With television's ubiquitous help, ordinary people are brought into vicarious contact with large areas of the world and can and do react quickly when their interests and emotions have been touched.

As a result, statesmen find they have to work the levers of public opinion to influence other countries because government-to-government channels are no longer enough. When George Bush pledged his support for Boris Yeltsin, he used the media to send his message directly to the Soviet people; the priority was to promote popular opposition to the coup. When television showed graphic pictures of Iraqi savagery against the Kurds, millions of U.S. and foreign viewers sent a message to Bush; he quickly reversed his own position and ordered American troops to the rescue. Disorderly mass politics increasingly replaces traditional diplomacy.

The candles in Moscow flickered with the memories of an extraordinary moment, extraordinary for the world as well as for the long-suffering Russian people. The waves of liberation that rose in Poland more than a decade earlier had finally reached shore in Moscow in August 1991. After seventy-four years, the revolution of Lenin and Stalin and the Soviet empire had collapsed. But the forces that produced these spectacular events were themselves part of a larger, still expanding revolution that engulfs all the world's peoples in accelerating technological change, social and political movement, and infinite tensions between soaring desires and lagging fulfillment, between free markets and economic justice.

Societies have entered the electronic age from different directions and different points of time, loaded down with their own histories, with myths inherited from earlier experiences. Yet they are all being subjected to the same rhythms of global change: instant communications and mass information, expanding consumer expectations, mingling cultures, mass movements, and migrating populations—millions upon millions of ordinary citizens and peasants, moving from the peripheries of public life into the centers. We can hear the roar of the crowd. People power on the rise and old ruling elites in retreat. Nationalities claiming their independence while national sovereignty slips down the slope of its own decline. We can feel the constant acceleration of life, the tremendous energies being released, the social fissures developing along the fault lines of other eras.

The rush of new communications technology is testing the very limits of social tolerance and adjustment, so there is, as William McNeill tells us, "a kind of race between the rational, disciplined, cooperative potentialities of human-kind, and the urge to destroy, which also lurks in every human psyche."[20] If the democratic surge is to be sustained and reason is to prevail over the urge to destroy, then knowledge must prevail over information and wisdom over mass TV emotions. A port of entry to knowledge and wisdom is an understanding of the communications revolution itself. As we shall see, this is a fascinating story.

II

The New Anatomy of Knowledge

REVOLUTIONS ARE LIKE CIRCLES. They have no beginnings and no ends, only the ceaseless flow of change from a past beyond memory to a future beyond imagination. Looking back, we can see the flowering of Greek culture or the fall of Rome, the age of exploration or the discovery of electricity, but these are merely the identifying marks of transition, like volcanic eruptions that occasionally remind us of the perpetual movement of magma beneath the earth's surface. Indeed, revolutions do not even exist except in the minds of the men and women who define them, usually in retrospect and according to the vagaries of contemporary intellectual fashion, yet in response to a general human need for labels to tell us where we are or where we have been.

The communications revolution, then, is an idea that defines a universe, a universe of change set in motion by the electronic extension of human knowledge and visual experience to nearly all the world's peoples within a single dimension of time and space. For the first time in history, the rich and poor, literate and illiterate, city worker and peasant farmer are linked together by shared images of global life, from local neighborhood to faraway city. They are buffeted by the same rush of new ideas and sensations, swept by the same tides of human disorder that mark our passage from one age to another.

Writing and the printing press were two of civilization's greatest inventions. But for speed, global reach, and deep social penetration, nothing can compare with the electronic wonders that have burst over us in just the last three or four decades. They are the ubiquitous messengers of contemporary life, the catalysts that initiate and magnify other revolutions. They even accelerate their own development, so that new inventions crowd into our lives in bewildering number and complexity. Today, TVs, computers, satellite networks, VCRs, faxes, DBS dishes, laser CDs, cellular radios, fiber optics, and multimedia systems. Tomorrow, interactive television, virtual reality, and artificial intelligence. A constant state of newness continuing to the end of imagination. Never-ending invention assaulting human psyches but extending the power of knowledge to ever more millions of individuals.

The boom in VCRs which began in the United States in the mid-1980s spread like a flash fire around the world and became a powerful weapon in the struggle between repression and freedom. Easily copied, smuggled, and sold through black markets, videos passed with ease through police controls. More than 10 million cassettes circulated in Poland before the overthrow of communism. "The VCR killed Ceauşescu even before his execution," says the scholar Vladimir Tismaneanu. "It was the most important factor in terms of creating a mass consciousness."[1] In mullah-dominated Iran, not even whippings and death sentences were able to stop the influx of subversive Western videos.

Advances were even more striking in computer technology. In just the last two decades, software speeds increased 3,000-fold while hardware improved by a factor of 1,000. Computers became the engines of modern production, marketing, and management; they were a principal factor in the growth of multinational corporations and the global economy. Rapidly shrinking size, complexity, and costs also moved computers into the range of office workers and homeowners, so that between 1983 and 1990 more than 113 million desktop and portable units were sold worldwide. Just as significant, computer and communications technologies were merging into common systems combining language and voice and moving pictures. All the dimensions of life converted into digital codes and instantly transported anywhere on earth. The buffers of time and space stripped away from experience so that human encounters would be more immediately and harshly felt.

But the most celebrated of the new technologies, of course, was television, which was an instant sensation as it spread rapidly from country to country during the last decades of the twentieth century. Only a novelty for Americans in the 1950s, it was a mind-numbing consumer of people's time by the 1970s. In the Soviet Union, there were just 10,000 TV sets in 1950, but by 1991, more than 80 percent of the population watched television every day. When I first went to China in 1975, a television set was a rare sight, but on another trip in 1988, I saw roofs festooned with TV aerials, and programs reached an astonishing 800 million viewers. By the 1990s, more homes in Rio de Janeiro had television than had running water. Bedouins watched Jordanian and even Israeli television in tents in the Sinai. In Papua New Guinea and the Himalayan kingdom of Bhutan state-of-the-art electronics kept citizens in touch with distant events. Pakistani farmers looked at TV commercials for tractors. Dish antennae blossomed in Indian cities, while cable systems exploded from 100 to more than 4,000 in just six years. "First there was one channel, then two, now six," says Rajiv Mehrotra, the young founder of a TV dish company. "People want nine channels now. It's precisely the same as the United States some 30 years ago."[2]

Television created strong new competition for newspapers, challenged the empire of movies, and broke radio's monopoly on broadcast news and entertainment. It became the favored source of information for most Americans and, as receivers became more available, for most of the rest of the world as well. For television is not just an offspring of radio, a distant relative of print, another page in media history that requires some social notice but no significant institutional adjustment. It is a unique phenomenon that is profoundly influencing everything we do—how we see the world, how we think, how we act, how we govern. It is altering our perceptions of reality and, together with computers, changing the very nature of the knowledge we acquire and use.

What sets television apart from all other forms of communication ever invented is its ability to transmit human experiences in real time over great distances with a visual power and motion that mimic life itself—that, indeed, can so intensify experience through the manipulation and repetition of images that the real world often suffers by comparison. The alphabet, as Marshall McLuhan observed, was a technology of fragmentation and specialization.[3] The printing press, says the print historian Elizabeth L. Eisenstein, promoted the standardization, preservation, and proliferation of knowledge.[4] The computer drives knowledge toward quantifiable data that can be measured, stored, and coded; it does not provide a kindly environment for abstract thought or those intuitive flights of imagination that produce Einstein theories and Watson-Crick models. Television uniquely sweeps knowledge across the barriers of literacy, transforming all of life into moving images and sensory stimuli. It creates impressions instead of ideas and emotions instead of thought. Just as the invention of writing destroyed the value of memory that Socrates championed, the electronic revolution devalues writing. Prodigious feats of remembering were no longer necessary when knowledge could be stored in a library. And now when the world can be seen on a screen, the need for writing is diminished. Reading and writing are skills that must be learned. Effort is required to translate ideas into words and then to convert words into the mental images and associations that trigger emotional responses and action. Television makes no such demands. It operates directly on the senses, harmonizing perfectly with the human preference for lazy ways.

Walter Lippmann, contemplating the silent movies seventy years ago, foresaw the authority that visual communication would exercise over words and imagination. "Photographs . . . seem utterly real," he observed in his classic *Public Opinion*. "They come, we imagine, directly to us without human meddling, and they are the most effortless food for the mind conceivable. Any description in words, or even any inert picture, requires an effort of memory before a picture exists in the mind. But on the screen the whole process of observing, describing, reporting, and then imagining has been accomplished for you."[5] Yet something far more profound than observing and reporting is involved now. For with television, the experience itself can be recorded in nearly all its immediate sensory effect and transmitted almost instantly to countless millions of viewers in every corner of the earth.

Words, however, are abstract symbols with no life of their own; language has no meaning until the mind makes the crucial connections between verbal codes and stored memories to create new pictures in the imagination. If you actually see a friend killed by a car, all your senses are instantly flooded with real sights and sounds. But if you only read about a friend's accident, the experience is quite different. Time and distance intervene; the event must be re-created in your imagination and your reactions reconstructed out of remembered associations and emotions. Inevitably, the effect is attenuated by an element of detachment.

It is this detachment from the senses that makes the printed word less involving than television, for it interposes the mind between living experience and emotional reactions. "Perhaps the most significant of the gifts of typography to man," said McLuhan, "is that of detachment and non-involvement—the power to act without reacting." This contributed, he said, to the principle of scholarly detachment, which became a guiding ideal of modern science.[6] The same separation of language from senses is also more congenial to deliberative thought and the reasoning process. In written communication, the imagination converts codes into a version of reality, and the mind reasons its way to judgments, convictions, and actions. With television, by contrast, movement, sound, and color rush experiences directly to the senses. The process moves from image to impression, to emotional impulse, and then to action. Sensation and emotional intensity dominate. The reflection and reasoning which verbal communication demands are bypassed.

Another profound difference between television and writing is the way they collect and disseminate knowledge. Television absorbs the scenes within the range of its lenses, records the images, then diffuses them like a gas. It creates the illusion of reproducing life in its natural, multidimensional state. Languages, by contrast, convert life into artificial codes and organize these into artificial patterns. Most languages, for example, are linear. Words, sentences, and thoughts troop across or down the page in a straight line. John Locke believed that ideas enter single file into the mind and only then mingle with other ideas or submit to manipulation by the imagination.[7] This single-file thinking seems to be not so much a product of nature as a consequence of the thought process's being bent artificially to fit the medium of language. "There is nothing linear or sequential about the total field of awareness that exists in any moment of consciousness," McLuhan observed. "Consciousness is not a verbal process."[8] The actual sensory world, in other words, is more closely approximated by TV images than by writing.

One effect of this linear bias of written language, and also of the grammar handed down from the Greeks and Romans, is that it promotes a kind of reasoning that arranges facts in sequences and operates on the logic of cause and effect.[9] This is of more than theoretical interest because the human mind is remade by its own tools, and language largely defines both the individual and his society. Differences in language and grammar go far to explain why two societies can look at exactly the same problem and run off in opposite directions. Over the centuries, for example, ideographic writing in East Asian cultures favored a very different thinking process than did Western phonetic alphabets. The Chinese philosopher Tung-sun Chang says Western philosophy is determined by Western grammar and Chinese philosophy by Chinese grammar.[10] Winston Churchill once suggested that the rigidity of Japanese military planning was "largely due to the cumbersome and imprecise nature of their language."[11] While Edwin O. Reischauer rejected the "canard" that Japanese is too lacking in clarity and logic to meet the demands of modern technology, he conceded that "probably it is easier to be ambiguous and vague in Japanese than in most Indo-European tongues."[12]

Even though these subtleties of communication do not make the evening news, they are crucial in shaping relations between societies. It is the mismatch between Western and Asian ways of thinking, for example, that has made a major contribution to the misunderstandings which have plagued the two civilizations for so many centuries. And this raises a fascinating question. Will differences be altered or diminished as television re-creates knowledge in its own image? More and more, the world's masses are seeing the world through the same kinds of lenses. Imitations of reality come to them in the same audiovisual form. This standardized communication operates across cultures and, in a sense, promotes a common way of seeing things. Whether this way is valid or invalid, it creates shared impressions that are independent of language. They are not bound to linear or ideographic thought—or perhaps any thought at all.

As TV images come to dominate words, the way knowledge is acquired and used changes. The texture of social and political intercourse is altered. Intense sensory experience becomes the common expectation, and electronic impressions are the connecting links of daily awareness. The evidence is everywhere. Picture-story reading methods a few years ago, and now TV teaching aids in elementary schools and remedial reading courses in colleges. Fifteen-second TV commercials and psychedelic videos. Strong graphic emphasis in everything from industrial design to TV-style newspapers like *USA Today*.

Computers that began as number crunchers and then word processors are now caught up in a graphics craze, with software keyed to screen icons and multicolored visuals and with mouse controls substituting for verbal codes. Video presentations are the rage from corporate boardrooms to international conferences. It is assumed that consumers need to be entertained to buy. But the same is true of CEOs who don't like to read long reports or think big thoughts. They prefer closed-circuit television and teleconferencing to keep tabs on far-flung operations. The chief actor at planning meetings is often a TV monitor flashing video demonstrations, glitzy graphs, and one-line slogans designed to sweep executives on to decisions without disturbing their mental faculties. The same oral-visual cult flourishes in the White House. In his kiss-and-tell book about the Reagan years, former Budget Director David A. Stockman remarked that Michael K. Deaver and his White House colleagues "never read anything. They lived off the tube."[13] And no one would accuse George Bush of being a reader like Harry Truman.

There are a number of reasons for television's extraordinary influence. One of the most important is the fact that it gives viewers the feeling they are eyewitnesses to the history passing before them on the screen. They have a sense of vicarious participation in events and a personal acquaintance with people in public life. They can see with their own eyes what is happening. The world comes to them directly in living color, neither altered by newspaper reporters nor muted by what Theodore H. White called the "filter of time."[14] There is an immediacy about the moving images, an intensity of directly felt experience, that holds power over written accounts of a remembered past. Thanks to Minicams, portable uplinks, global satellite networks, and the nearly universal availability of TV sets, pictures can be transmitted to worldwide audiences while fires are still burning and tragedies unfolding. So we see Haitian survivors struggling in the water after their boat has sunk or hungry Kurds fighting over bundles of emergency food being dropped by helicopters in frozen Anatolian mountains. And what grips our emotions is not simply the dramatic scenes. It is the realization that we are watching real people fighting for their lives. And we are watching them now, seemingly while they are still struggling, rather than reading about them hours later in the morning paper.

These simulations of a raw present are beyond anything that newsreels or films could deliver. Despite the glorification of movies, their reach was always limited by their physical dependence on theater houses and their need to charge admission. In the case of news, they were also handicapped by the slowness of their technology. Newsreels were so stale by the time they were seen by audiences that even the hyped narration and music of *The March of Time* could not make them seem fresh. One day in the spring of 1919, for example, a movie camera was rolling when more than 3,000 college students massed in front of the great Gate of Heavenly Peace in Beijing, screaming their outrage over anti-Chinese provisions in the Treaty of Versailles, demanding democracy and freedom for their country, and clashing with police. The demonstration marked the beginning of the famous May Fourth Movement. It was an eerie, almost mystically accurate premonition of demonstrations that would take place seventy years later in Tiananmen Square. But there was a difference: the film produced by the unknown cameraman in 1919, which still survives, had no sound and little audience. By contrast, the television coverage in 1989 was broadcast live to a worldwide audience, generating waves of revulsion that ultimately congealed into international condemnation.

In the coverage of great natural occurrences and some defining moments in history, television can be a superb reporter. Remember the joyous flood of East Germans streaming through the Berlin Wall on an incredible night in 1989? Or earlier, when the space shuttle *Challenger* and seven astronauts suddenly disappeared in forked clouds of white gas over the Atlantic? An experience immediately felt by the millions who were watching when the explosion occurred and shared by other millions around the earth when the plumes of death were shown repeatedly in thousands of replayed broadcasts. Also, recall the moon walk? When for the first time human beings were able to see themselves from another astronomical body and realize that their earth is only a mote in the universe and not its center as tradition and religion taught. In 1990, *Intelsat* relayed the World Cup soccer matches to earth stations in fifty countries, sending 2 billion fans into a frenzy of shared enthusiasm. And in 1989, of course, the whole world watched as one shock followed another in a chain of upheavals that collapsed the Soviet empire and ended the Cold War.

Yet even in its finest moments, television can only imitate reality. The world it offers is artificial. Although TV watching is an act of sensory involvement, viewers cannot touch the people they see nor can anchors and newsmakers step out of TV sets for a tête-à-tête with viewers. In TV talk shows, which became such a prominent feature of the 1992 presidential election campaigns, viewers and stars can develop a kind of two-way exchange that resembles an ordinary conversation. But there still is no physical interaction, because mass television, for all its capabilities, is a medium that stands between viewers and performers. A person who sees a bomb about to explode on the screen does not run out of the house to save his life. The scene projects a sense of fear, and this is felt, but it is a transferred emotion that does not trigger the same surge of epinephrine as a personal threat. The images on the screen are only bodiless reflections, like the shadows on Plato's cave.

They are also distorted reflections, because television is like a carnival mirror. Except in some cases of live coverage, it twists reality out of its natural shape to serve the needs of drama more than truth. The problem is that the actual world is too large, too chaotic, too confusing, and, especially, too dull for television. The adventures of humanity must be converted into a form of entertainment. The emphasis is on strong visuals and lots of sound, brain-battering rock during brief interludes between violent action and sound bite reporting or dramatic dialogue. Powerful stimuli are manufactured to jangle nerves and quicken pulses; viewers must be kept in a state of high excitement or they might switch to another channel. It is feeling that counts, not ideas; things that can be seen rather than those that can only be imagined. In the case of news, producers pick through the daily welter of conflict, violence, and suffering, extract the most promising snippets of visual excitement, and then fashion these into short bursts of sight and sound. Stories are condensed into bundles of such concentrated drama that TV re-creations often appear larger than the events on which they are based. And the scenes singled out for viewing may be felt more fully by strangers in distant cities than by people standing in the center of the action.

During the Kremlin coup, for example, most Muscovites going to and from work or waiting in line at a *gastronom* saw ordinary backgrounds while foreigners saw only sensational foregrounds. The audiences of CNN got a closer view of the coup events than the people who were supposedly experiencing them. It was only later, when TV documentaries appeared on programs like *Vzglyad,* that Russians were exposed to the dramatic action they had missed. In the same way, print reporters are frequently surprised to see the dull confusion of stories they have covered magically transformed by TV producers into gems of emotional power and simplicity. This recalls an experience that Elaine Sciolino had when she covered the Iranian revolution for *Newsweek.* There were wild celebrations all over Teheran. The streets were crowded with people, cheering, dancing, and throwing flowers. She filed a color story with a festive spin to it and then dropped around to a television network bureau. She wanted a friend to show her what pictures they had in case she had missed something. She had. There on the videotape was a correspondent doing a standup in front of a burning building and talking about turbulent waves of screaming revolutionaries. "It must have been the only burning building in Teheran," she said. "But it gave them the drama they wanted."[15] The picture of the burning building was true, but the story it told was false.

The fact that the story was false in no way lessened the impact of the image, however, because illusions write as much history as fact and certainly more than truth, which is seldom found until after misunderstanding and folly have done their work. A false report of a student's death helped trigger the massive public revolt against Czechoslovakia's communist government in 1989. Michael Zantowsky, Vaclav Havel's press secretary, who was then a Reuters correspondent, got a report from a Civic Forum activist that a student had been beaten to death by riot police during a protest in downtown Prague. Zantowsky flashed the word to his news agency; this was quickly picked up by the Voice of America and relayed back into Czechoslovakia. "This incident probably as much as anything else caused huge demonstrations on November 20—about 200,000 people," Zantowsky recalled. "That started the whole thing and got the ball rolling." Secret police actually had staged the "death" to trick students into reporting it on their news service so there would be a pretext to shut the service down. But the stunt backfired. When the communists vehemently denied the report, no one believed them. And by the time facts caught up with error, Czechoslovakia had become a free nation.[16]

Wars also have been fought in the defense of illusions—

Vietnam comes immediately to mind—and nations have been based on myths like the declaration that "all men are created equal," which America's founding fathers proclaimed while they practiced slavery. What makes television special is its power to create and to destroy myths, to convert myth into reality or reality into myth, and to do these things with incredible speed on a global scale. One of the great legends of 1989 began when a man in a white shirt stood alone before a column of tanks on Chang An Jie in Beijing and raised his arm to signal a halt. "Was it by accident that the tank-stopper took his stand near the Beijing Hotel?" asked a *New York Times* TV critic. "The students were worldly enough to realize that their cause was made for television."[17] In the presence of bravery, it was a cruel question to ask—probably also irrelevant. For whether the scene was staged or not, television made it a universal reality, playing and replaying the tape for days on thousands of channels in every part of the planet. An unknown civilian was instantly transformed into an international icon of defiance. He became a legend just as Boris Yeltsin became a legend while standing on a tank. By focusing tightly on the man and the tank, television made it seem that Yeltsin was leading millions in the fight for democracy when only 200 or so supporters had mustered around him at the time. Most Russians stood on the sidelines during the crisis, but the illusion of mass defiance was taken as fact; the appearance of triumph became the reality of victory.

In addition to creating illusions of reality that can be more intensely felt than actual experience, television can move segments of life from one dimension of time to another so that, in effect, it rearranges reality. Just as a granddaughter's ballet lesson could be immortalized by a home video for future viewing by the Gorbachevs (and now by historians), so can public events be filmed, saved, and replayed again.

Not only does television supply references to the past, as newspapers and journals do, but in its own illusory way it returns the past to the present. People do not have to recall something that has happened; they can relive the experience through its electronic re-creation. An example is the now-famous eighty-one-second video of the four Los Angeles cops beating a black motorist. That vignette of brutality shocked Americans as no newspaper story could and started a chain of events that led eventually to riots, bloodshed, and the deployment of 5,000 federal troops. In a similar way, historic events can be brought to life. The film of the assassination of John F. Kennedy, for example, can stir emotions—and controversy—even among young people, who have no personal memories to resurrect. Television does the living for them through artful film editing, dramatic narration, and pulse-quickening music.

Televised repetition, sometimes incessant repetition of powerful sensations, is something else that can pile emotion upon emotion until the cumulative human response is greater than the initial reaction. The stream of violent scenes from the front lines of the American civil rights movement during the 1960s—freedom marchers being attacked by fire hoses, snarling police dogs, and "Bull" Connor's cattle prods—aroused the long-dormant consciences of whites and mobilized mass support for the most far-reaching civil rights legislation in the nation's history. Scenes of burning villages in Vietnam, children scalded by napalm, the summary execution of a man in a Saigon street—pictures endlessly duplicated and repeated—helped to end the war and destroy Lyndon Johnson. During the Gulf war, the process was reversed. Most of the savagery was kept off-screen; the viewing world saw primarily an air war. Ground-level scenes of destruction and human misery evoked strong reactions but only fleetingly because the coverage was so limited and the war so short. There was not enough visual carnage to incite an emotional uprising among viewers.

Still another of television's extraordinary accomplishments is the extension of existential knowledge beyond all previous horizons. Unending streams of living images now move silently, quickly, and effortlessly through the labyrinthine passages of the world's many cultures. They easily bypass the barriers of reading and restricted personal mobility to open up new human perspectives on an unprecedented scale. For the first time, nearly all the world's masses are being exposed to the globe-circling news, ideas, fads, and trends that are driving modern civilization. "In the traditional society the ideas one has, the beliefs one accepts, the arts one beholds are all within a bounded space," Daniel Bell observes. "Modernity bursts the walls. Everything is now available. Hindu mantras and Tantric mandalas, Japanese prints and African sculptures, Latin music and Indian ragas all jostle with one another in 'real time.' . . . All that we once knew played out on the scale of the Greek polis is now played out in the dimensions of the entire world."[18] A kind of global culture is emerging that, S. Frederick Starr notes, is far more Western at the moment than many Third World critics admit. As an example, he tells how Western musical scales and, broadly speaking, chord structures and meters have "fundamentally undermined the traditional aural environment of most of the world's peoples." Except for holdouts like the Arab Middle East, he says, "communications have not simply integrated musical languages but actually spread Western musical languages. Africa, for example, is dancing to American/Caribbean/European melodies and rhythms even as it (to some extent) reworks them under the influence of local practice. It is an amazing development."[19]

Indeed, the number of real and vicarious interactions between people has expanded beyond all previous limits. During the Middle Ages, scholars estimate that the average person saw no more than a hundred people in a lifetime. "The opportunity to become famous," says Gerald Clarke, "was granted only to the monarch, the pope, and perhaps a saint or two." People had to see Washington and Jefferson in person to know what they looked like; famous people only became famous faces as well as names after the invention of photography in the mid-nineteenth century.[20] Until very recent times, a Chinese peasant typically lived in a tiny circle of existence, surrounded by the terraced hills on which he worked, battered by nature, interacting with members of his family and a few villagers, but only vaguely aware of an outside world that came to him mostly through rumor and myth passed along by word of mouth. His knowledge was elemental; his reality reached no farther than the edges of the land where the sun rose and set.

In the cities of China, the standard greeting is *"Ni hao ma"* or "Are you well?" But what you can still hear in some rural areas is *"Chi le ma"* or "Have you eaten?"—a reminder of former centuries of famine, flood, and hardship. These tragedies never touched the sensibilities of other people because they were only vaguely known and not felt. At the time primitive communications kept the world in isolation wards that severely limited social contact. During the great Northwest China famine of 1929, more than 3 million people died. Yet Edgar Snow, who saw "thousands of men, women, and children starving to death before my very eyes," observed that it was "hardly noticed in the Western world, and even in the cities of China."[21]

It is very different now. When thousands of people are starving to death in Somalia, they are seen on television screens all over the world. Millions of viewers are exposed to the terrible scenes—children too weak even to cry, with bloated bellies and empty, staring eyes, slowly dying in their mothers' arms. Public emotions are aroused in many countries, and relief efforts are launched that, even if often frustrated, demonstrate a level of global awareness that was impossible in 1929. Through instant communications people living great distances from one another are joined in time and space by immediately shared experiences. Global life is turned on with a switch.

Stretching the limits of sensory experience beyond village sunrises and sunsets does not merely extend a farmer's horizons; it also alters his relationship to the world and the world's relationship to him. Bankers in Frankfurt or politicians in Washington are similarly affected by expanding experience because everyone is changed when the equations of knowledge are revised. The reason is that, to an important degree, a person defines himself by his environment. The experiences he has, the things he knows, the sights and sounds arriving in his consciousness every day are the bearings that locate him in the scheme of things. When these bearings are shifted by a whole galaxy of new sensations, he is thrust into a new life setting, and this is profoundly unsettling. For, as the scholar Colin Cherry observes, a person builds emotional walls around himself "not so much to keep others out as to contain himself, his kind, and his identity."[22] By penetrating these walls, modern communications change his self-perception. A Shanghai lathe operator going to work on a bicycle feels diminished when he sees pictures of Korean workers riding around in cars and striking whenever they have a grievance. Albanians watching high-living cats being served food on a silver platter in Italian TV commercials suddenly feel far worse off than they had thought and seize a ship to take them to a better life. A sense of personal identity that is fairly secure in a static time becomes uncertain and confused when the visual cues of life are multiplying and changing with bewildering speed.

Television affects personal perceptions in another way because it is an essentially passive form of communication. Viewing is an act of personal receiving rather than social exchange. No one needs to venture into the streets or a town square to be in touch with the world. It might be refreshing sometimes to go to a ballpark or an open-air concert, but this certainly is not necessary and it is often inconvenient. The Czech pianist Rudolf Firkusny recalls that when he was young attending a concert was a "tremendously important affair, almost like a holiday." But now, he says, "we can go home and listen to everything Beethoven or Chopin ever wrote with no effort at all. If we are not careful, music can lose its meaning."[23] There is little sociability even in the family living room. Parents and children may all be accounted for physically but remain in their own separate worlds. "Centered in the television set they are unaware of one another," says the French thinker Jacques Ellul. "It is no longer necessary for the members of a family to have anything at all to do with one another or even to be conscious of the fact that family relations are impossible."[24]

By drawing people into screen-lit living rooms, television does something else that has immense social and political implications. It tends to pull them out of neighborhoods and communities. The most distant events are delivered directly to the stuffed couch, to be consumed with fast-food dinners and large helpings of drama and sports, so there is a pulsating sense of the world at large. But outside the screen's glare, immediate surroundings sink into the darkness; it becomes an effort to get to know one's neighbors, even if they only live in the apartment down the hall. "The radio, and television even more than the radio, shuts up the individual in an echoing mechanical universe in which he is alone," Ellul observes. "He already knew little enough about his neighbors, and now the separation between him and his fellows is further widened. . . . No more face-to-face encounters, no more dialogue."[25] So the inner circle of human awareness shrinks while the outer circle expands. The viewing ritual itself helps determine how knowledge is acquired and also, therefore, what kind of knowledge is retained.

Still another critical fact about electronic knowledge is volume. As late as the 1950s, sportswriters were filing game stories by telegraph at forty words a minute. Wire service Teletype machines operated at only sixty-five words a minute. Telephone systems were primitively slow. Television news was in its infancy. Life's horizons were relatively limited. But then with the onrush of new technology, the picture quickly changed. Stunning advances in computers, television, and communication speeds, capacity, and range produced an explosion of new sensations and information. Both the sources of existential knowledge, from videotapes to cable TV outlets, and the amount of transmitted knowledge expanded exponentially, doubling and quadrupling many times over. It did not matter whether there was any need for more news or commentaries or business messages or bank transfers or meaningless data or red tape or chitchat. The fact that a fax seemed more urgent than a letter or a video news release was more glamorous than a typewritten handout did not make them more necessary. The *Encyclo- paedia Britannica* could be transmitted in less than a minute, but why? Because the technology was there; it had to be used. That is the law of the technological age. So, like garbage in a landfill, information refuse accumulates as fast as communications expand, and this is called progress.

Images swim by in endless profusion, fires and plane crashes, statesmen and demagogues, controversies and violence, comedies, crime shows, and docudramas, popular protests and crumbling rulers, weather and sports. Visual impressions, immediate and global, running pell-mell through one's consciousness. One set of fast-cut scenes no sooner arriving than they are replaced by another. Commercials reduced to an incomprehensible staccato of light and noise. Fads spinning in and out of focus. News stories speeding by in a blur. Iran-Contra . . . housing program ripoffs . . . savings and loan scandals . . . the Gulf war . . . the coup in Moscow . . . pictures of Bosnian wounded and starving Somalis one week, and the bodies of Bangladeshi flood victims the next.

In the process, human circuits become overloaded: too many impressions to absorb, too many things to react to. Food donations to starving refugees in Africa fell off in 1991, aid workers reported, because Westerners were suffering from "donor fatigue." They couldn't cope with any more misery that year. But more pictures and mass guilt in 1992 set off new waves of public outrage and demands for humanitarian action in the cases of Somalia and Bosnia. The floods of sensory stimuli may be electronic and the images artificially created. Some impressions may even be false, as we noted earlier, but they arrive in the human emotion center in the guise of reality. And this reality, magnified and emotionalized by the mass media, can become unbearable. An effort to escape the pressures of modernity is one reason cited for the rise of interest in religion, ethnicity, pop psychology, and meditative movements like Zen. For as T. S. Eliot observed, humankind cannot bear very much reality.[26]

In these chaotic conditions, the stability of knowledge is upset. Phenomenal increases in speed and volume, added to the sensory bias of televised communication, increase the volatility of the impressions from which attitudes and opinions are formed. The raw material of the mind becomes more and more evanescent, with images flickering for only an instant on the screen of consciousness, then becoming lost in new sensations. The capacity for focus, concentration, clarity, and rational deliberation is impaired or lost altogether. The pressures on values and beliefs are increased.

These developments, touching the genetic codes of human identity and intercourse, are centered first in the individual but, gathered together, become the expression of a whole society, establishing its view of the world and changing its collective set of mind. When sensations dominate thought and feelings substitute for deliberation, they deny wisdom its place in both personal and public affairs. When the process of knowing is altered by the medium of knowing, then life itself is changed because knowledge is its mold. Although language, writing, and printing are their own lasting monuments to human progress, their influence is diminished in an electronic age of incessant noise and emotional clutter.

Every advance in knowledge and technique marks indelibly the ages it dominates. This is particularly true in the case of communication, which is the central nervous system of human organization and endeavor. Fundamental to what is happening today is the intimate relationship that exists—and always has existed—between communications technology and civilization.

III

The Global Spread of Mass Societies

ANOTHER TRANSFORMING PHENOMENON of the electronic age is the rapid formation and global spread of modern mass societies. The same technologies that are changing the dimensions of personal life are also expanding the boundaries of society far beyond anything seen before. People living in separate clusters scattered across large landmasses are now being drawn into integrated social networks by real-time contacts and by a new common base of shared sensations, experiences, and information. Truly national societies, once limited to a few countries, are now forming along a broad front.

The paradox of these societies is that the mass is the product of the singular; it is an infinitude of personal attitudes, feelings, and opinions, individual connections and private reactions to vicarious experiences imported from near and far. Whereas industrial society submerged the person in the machine, electronic mass society singles him out, making the individual the basic unit of social attention and coherence. In the process, old patterns focused on family and community yield to self-centered personal concerns. And the society that emerges is a collection of individual parts rather than one organism with a unified organizing principle.

The bias is toward the individual because that is the bias of communications technology. And to a remarkable degree, this is what is writing the specifications of the new world emerging around us. Societies are not simply being expanded; they are being changed fundamentally. Technology is imposing its own templates on the relationships among people. The nationalizing of cultures, the explosive spread of consumerism, revolutions of rising expectations, and the breakdown of internal and external isolation, within nations and between great civilizations, are just a few of the social trends that bear the marks of the communications revolution.

Although nation-states have existed for a long time, truly national societies are a relatively recent arrival. For most of their history, Americans were organized around small farms and individual communities, connected by railroad and telegraph, to be sure, but otherwise centered on their own local interests, leaders, and newspapers. In time, however, cars and airplanes increased mobility, cities sprawled out into suburbs, industries expanded, and jobs migrated. First radio and then television linked communities from coast to coast in an all-embracing world of entertainment, information, and advertising. While newspapers remained local and regional, television became the greatest nationalizing force in American history. Local and regional divisions began breaking down. Never fully but enough to create instant national images, celebrities, fads, news, and public issues. Nuclear power or abortion, any subject capable of raising emotions, was moved quickly to the national screen by the networks. Thought and comment were standardized, despite a proliferation of supposedly diverse channels and programming.

Local sports stars and teams were repackaged as national programs. Local pulpits were huckstered into national TV ministries. Hundreds of breweries, once bastions of local taste and loyalty, died in the rush of corporations to national brands and network advertising.

Thanks to improved communications, corporations could put large manufacturing, distribution, and marketing operations on a national platform. Independent local grocers and bakers with old-fashioned community roots were expendable; national sales organizations and supermarket outlets were more efficient. Communities lost their distinguishing marks in look-alike malls. Television commercials guided life and living, what to eat, what to wear, how to exercise, where to vacation. Social patterns took on the colors of the media's world. Consumption became an American passion. Advertising pressured individuals not just to fill needs but to seek all the other good things in life that industry could promote and they could imagine. "Selling became the most striking activity of contemporary America," Daniel Bell has observed. "Against frugality, selling emphasized prodigality; against asceticism, the lavish display."[1] Even people with no money felt the urge to spend. More and more, they measured their success by new cars and TV aerials. The cumulative result was a revolution of rising expectations. Yearnings for necessities became desires for luxuries; past wants became present demands. And the psychology of affluence and self-indulgence became a prominent feature of national life.

Although Americans moved sooner and more deeply into the electronic revolution than most other societies and although some of their responses may have been culture-specific, the fundamental forces at work were not unique. Similar nationalizing trends have developed in many other countries as they have fallen increasingly under the influence of modern mass communications. In Russia, television was a nonstarter until the 1970s and 1980s, but then it became a national obsession. Despite dreary programming, viewers proved to be as addicted as Americans; the Russian couch potato index in 1992 showed an average family watching TV more than six hours a day. Many of the same social patterns also appeared: a significant falloff in reading, schoolchildren spending more time watching than studying, a drop in moviegoing, lower attendance at concerts and similar events, less participation in sports, and a decline in radio listening.

Ellen Mickiewicz, a leading analyst of Russian society, has called television's impact nothing less than revolutionary. "It is the medium that has created the first mass public in Soviet history," she says. "It is a public that embraces the barely literate and the academician, the hero mothers of Central Asia and the engineers of Sverdlovsk."[2] With television, ideas, fads, issues, and controversies traveled quickly across eleven time zones and through the country's many cultures. As always, people continued to be preoccupied with their immediate affairs—family, work, illness, and other directly felt experiences. But television put their lives in the context of the larger world. They could relate their experiences to what was happening to other people in other communities and countries. People were not homogenized, as Professor Mickiewicz is quick to emphasize; regional and ethnic differences not only did not magically disappear but in many cases were exacerbated. But millions of viewers everywhere found themselves looking at their neighbors, country, and world through the same electronic lenses. After glasnost especially, the whole country shared in reports of national disasters, interviews with foreign leaders, talk shows, and live coverage of parliamentary debates. Even propaganda and censorship could not prevail against the power of pictures. Long-isolated layers of society were

linked—if not fused—by a chain of common images traveling over national and regional networks. However variously
they might react, people were being exposed on a very large
scale to similar events, ideas, and trends.

With a major assist from urbanization and rising educational levels, even the historic divide between city and farm
was narrowed. "Thanks to modern communications," says
William H. McNeill, ". . . the sharp gap that once prevailed
between what rural folk knew and experienced and what
urban populations knew and experienced has been drasti-
cally reduced. This constitutes the most fundamental social
and political change wrought by the technological transfor-
mations of the 20th Century, and its consequences within
the Soviet Union are only part of a much wider global
phenomenon."[3]

Evidence of this can be found in many countries but most
remarkably, perhaps, in China, where from time im-
memorial and into modern times the peasant masses, like
the serfs in feudal Europe, have lived in the outback of their
own civilization. They have never been a ruling force, despite the peasant origins and pretensions of Mao's communism. In the past, when it was easier to control information,
political leaders could keep one group isolated from another.
But now news and information move indiscriminately
among both the privileged and the unprivileged. Different
segments of society are more directly and immediately connected. Not only are many of the peasants far better off than
in older times but they are much better informed about
what is going on in China and the outside world. At the time
of the prodemocracy demonstrations in 1989, the noted
Chinese journalist Liu Binyan observed that the passive
attitude of the Chinese people, *including* the peasants, had
finally changed after thousands of years. He cited in particular the "very important phenomenon" of peasants organiz-

ing "self-governing" bodies at the grass-roots level in places like Hebei and Shandong provinces.[4] This activism was accompanied by a heightened political awareness, which television promoted, and closer ties between different groups, which improved horizontal communications, made possible. "All of the technology of communication has become much more readily available to common citizens," says Andrew Walder. "It's not monopolized by the party or by work units, in the way that it was in a previous era." The result is that there is now "a much better capacity to act, organize and communicate."[5]

In the process of binding large populations and disparate cultures into highly interactive relationships, the communications revolution has also promoted a surging consumerism that is another defining characteristic of modern mass societies. The whole thrust of the mass media—from mass marketing to mass entertainment and including a great deal of news coverage—is to sell individuals on the values of maximum consumption and the satisfaction of personal desires. It has been widely assumed that the United States holds the exclusive franchise for conspicuous consumption; this is attributed to a national character defect which, in the presence of affluence, produces self-indulgent materialism rather than refined European taste. But, as W. W. Rostow has argued, other nations also move on to the heights of "high mass consumption" and "consumer sovereignty" when their economies are able to supply more than the basics of food, shelter, and clothing.[6] "Foreign criticism," *The Economist* concedes, "often attacks American habits that the critics themselves happily adopt a few years later."[7] Supposedly superior cultures seem to develop the same weakness for self-indulgence when they are exposed to the same base influences of media hype.

Few nations have worked more zealously to separate

themselves from the encroachments of Western consumerism than India. Its intellectuals rail against America's cultural imperialism, but the ravages of Western-style television, films, and advertising are taking their toll. "No matter what product is offered these days to India's burgeoning middle class—soda water, clothes, cigarettes, computers," one observer reports, "the inspiration for its advertising is the same: to live abroad, free as a bird, and get rich in the bargain."[8] Despite a long-cultivated anti-Americanism, the United States is today's "dream destination" for India's yuppies and puppies (Punjabi urban professionals). The same consumer fever has spread to farmers in the once isolated rural areas of India, where manufacturers are finding a burgeoning new market for middle-class luxuries. "We find that the Indian farmer has a lot of money to spare," says Parag Maholikar, a market researcher. "The electronic media has really played havoc. They are reaching 30 percent of rural households. They carry the latest lifestyles and products for daily use. . . . This has raised the expectations of rural folks and they are trying to emulate their brothers, the urban folks." Even the harijans or untouchables have been affected. "I don't go to the shops," said one woman, "but the younger daughters or daughters-in-law go. I use a neem twig to brush my teeth, but my children use Colgate."[9]

Another supposedly resistant culture is Japan. It is cited approvingly as a contrast to the United States—a wealthy society where strong national character stands guard against the cultural degradations of mass consumption. Yet the former executive director of the giant Japanese advertising firm Dentsu, Fujioka Wakao, writes about "learning to live the good life" and cites a new life-style that says, "I want to sample one exotic new delicacy after another."[10] The new rich and the new poor have joined in a common cause: "to consume as never before."[11] Credit cards have become the rage in Japan, with the number of users, the size of debt carried, and personal bankruptcy rates all rising much faster than in the United States.[12] "Contrary to popular misconception," says the Hakuhodo Institute of Life and Living, Japanese workers "are not ants slaving away for the company at the expense of their private lives and families."[13]

Similar consumer forces have gathered momentum in other fast-advancing countries around the Pacific Rim. As *Fortune* put it in a special survey: Asians have become serious consumers as a result of a series of trends bound together and impelled by the "unceasing, accelerating global exchange of information."[14] In Indonesia, for example, the middle classes have been expanding rapidly, buying homes and cars on time and using credit cards with almost as much abandon as Americans. Newspapers advertise such frivolities as dog vitamins. Glitzy consumer palaces, including one called Blok M. Plaza in a suburb of Jakarta, display the latest women's fashions in shops with names like Yupporium. Everywhere, it seems, the imperatives of new consumerism and media stimulation will not be frustrated by old cultures.

In China, of all places, not only is the culture of conspicuous consumption flourishing in booming east coast provinces but the government itself is promoting the very capitalist consumerism it denounces. State television sells commercials to supplement its budget, and these advertise everything from beauty aids and home furnishings to herbal medicine and Chinese Roto-Rooters. Five, ten, or more spots, many with foreign sponsors, are bunched together in a program segment, packed with sales-stimulating music and graphics and pitched directly to consumers. Although these spots do not yet come close to the commercial blitzes inflicted on Westerners, they are a hint that China, despite its cultural uniqueness, will be bent like other societies to the laws of mass information and mass marketing. For the commercials promote a consumerist psychology that cannot be controlled the way information was before the electronic age. They stimulate personal expectations that exacerbate social disillusionment if they are not satisfied. However helpful exciting pictures of new goods may be to Deng's "four modernizations," they do not promote individual satisfaction if they only dramatize what a Chinese worker in Xiamen has and a peasant in Anhui or Qinghai does not, or what other nations have and China lacks. Also, because commercials focus on the individual and involve personal choice, they attack the very core of Chinese society, which traditionally treats individuals as only anonymous members of an amorphous mass.

As all these trends suggest, the rapid modernization of societies is a traumatic experience. Lives are rushed into new circumstances too fast for personal orientation or institutional adjustment. Floods of new technology and information enlarge human experience but also increase complexity and anxiety. In the very act of nationalizing societies, mass communications generate enormous stresses that can play havoc with those societies. This is revealed in a number of ways.

One is the saturation of life with desires for more goods and personal services than economies or governments can satisfy. In the United States, runaway consumerism produced a revolution of rising expectations that escalated into a revolution of entitlements, in which desires were defined as rights. This helped to fuel the social upheavals of the 1960s and led to a historic expansion of mandated public services.[15] As challenging as the American expectations were, however, they were addressed to a strong economy; consumer demands could be matched at least in part by the output of goods and services. It is more dangerous to light such consumer fuses in less productive countries. Then the gap between aspiration and realization becomes unmanageably wide, and social breakdowns threaten peaceful transitions to modernity. Unfortunately, says Gopal Saksena of India's Doordarshan Television, TV commercials project a better life than people in a developing society can afford, so they end by creating "a feeling of frustration and inferiority."[16]

This was exactly the feeling of the Russian people in the 1970s and 1980s, when they became painfully aware of the modern conveniences that were flooding through Western lives while they were still condemned to shoddy products and monumental shortages. Formerly resigned to the basic necessities of life, they began demanding the same cornucopia of goods, the same variety and quality that capitalism offered. When state industries failed miserably to deliver, popular dissatisfaction grew, and this was an important contributing factor in the eventual downfall of the communist system. After the downfall, however, the psychology worked in reverse. Free-market economics became the rallying cry of Boris Yeltsin and his reformers, but sausages did not magically appear on store shelves; results did not begin to catch up with public anticipation. Popular discontents deepened, as they had so many times before in Russia, but this time the complaints were centered on new democratic ideas rather than on old communist ideologies. The mass marketing of mass marketing only increases social tensions when it escalates popular expectations beyond possible realization.

Another way in which the social stresses of modernization reveal themselves is the ethnic and religious activism now so prominently displayed around the world. During a period of unprecedented global integration, there is curiously an epidemic of tribalism. The earth is littered with ancient animosities, seemingly incurable hatreds that set race against race, tribe against tribe, and religion against religion.

Blacks and whites in South Africa, Armenians and Azerbaijanis in the Transcaucasus, Serbs, Croats, and Moslems in Yugoslavia, and Hindus and Moslems in India. Although many complex elements are obviously involved, the present surge of tribalism is, to an important degree, a defensive mechanism—masses of people reacting against the unsettling intrusions of modern life. "It is this very pressure toward homogeneity created by national television and faster crossing of space," says Daniel Bell, "that leads people to recoil and seek for more primordial attachments in localism and smaller national breakaways."[17] Nowhere is this more evident than in the Middle East, where much of the turbulence can be traced to cultural factors like religion, ethnic anger, and the group psychology that develops when civilizations are ground between two ages like wheat between millstones. More than oil or Western "imperialism," it is humiliation over an inability to compete with Western societies that underlies much that we have seen in the Arab world during last fifty years. Islamic fundamentalism is not so much a rush to Allah as a flight into a mystic past to escape from a failed present.

Social fractures also develop in advanced industrial nations, where mass communications increase personal proximity and intensify perceptions of personal disparity. For American whites living their own lives far from Harlem or south-central Los Angeles, television provides not only hard pictorial evidence of historic injustice and unsolved social contrasts but also vivid impressions of underclass crime and drugs. For blacks, by contrast, daily images of white affluence and indulgence, appearing in everything from soap operas to TV commercials, are a powerful visualization of their own relative exclusion in a supposedly egalitarian society. "Through television," says the scholar Joshua Meyrowitz, "today's ghetto children have more points of reference and higher standards for comparison. They see what they are being deprived of in every program and commercial."[18] Feelings of difference are intensified when actual disadvantage is combined with dramatic media portrayals of better alternatives in life.

In the same way, private frustrations increase when rising expectations encounter descending possibilities. It is in these circumstances that individuals lose faith in government and the general society, and seek support in the more familiar precincts of church and ethnic group. African-Americans, full of rage over unfulfilled hopes, turned to their own deeply religious culture for shared identity and communal strength. They organized their strivings for a better life around ministers like Martin Luther King, Jr. Many turned to Islam and, with it, adopted Arabic names such as Muhammad Ali or Kareem Abdul-Jabbar. They looked beyond the white society they saw on television to Africa to find the origins of a separate and distinguishing identity. Similar defensive mechanisms can be seen at work in other societies. From Quebec to Fiji, group frustrations are being acted out in many forms of ethnic, religious, and cultural separatism.

One of the memorable scenes that marked the fall of communism in Russia was the mingling of church and state in the final hours of the coup and the ceremonial transfers of power. There was an Orthodox priest leading prayers at the Russian White House during the height of danger. Then Boris Yeltsin and a huge crowd attending mass in Epiphany Cathedral. Many young people in the streets were wearing crosses. A young Ph.D. explained that they wanted to demonstrate their repudiation of communism, but others said it was more than that. Polls showed that organized religion was the most trusted institution in the country. Many Russians were looking to the church for values to fill spiritual voids and for personal bearings in a time of enormous social stress. When Vladimir Molchanov, the highly respected producer of the TV show *Before and After Midnight,* was asked why he was developing a religious news program, he replied: "Because it's very important. There are more religious people in Russia than there are communists."[19]

Another source of stress is the velocity of social change, which collapses the time for transitions. New patterns of life—new perspectives, expectations, frustrations, and confusions—develop faster than old ones can be discarded. Economic trends and social demands race ahead of slow-moving institutions. While the United States spent more than half a century making the historic journey from a rural to an urban mass society, many nations today are being catapulted from one age to another without the buffer of time. Their adjustment process is infinitely more traumatic. Especially so in a country like China, where an agrarian-industrial shift that once might have taken several centuries is being compressed into decades. Even slight increases in the rate of migration from countryside to city can produce momentous social problems, as Cairo and Mexico City demonstrate. The prospect in a land of one billion people is mind-boggling. Yet it is television's nature to speed change, not to slow it, to stimulate rather than to retard the formation of modern societies.

The mass communications revolution not only is creating these societies, however, but also is binding them to one another in a vast tangle of relationships that are, quite literally, creating a new kind of global civilization. With the development of communications satellites, computers, and long-range jets, the networking of information, technology, marketing, and production rapidly spread beyond national borders to encompass most of the earth. Transnational corporations expanded explosively, both in the range of their operations and in the influence they exercised over global trends. The lives of people in different countries and in different stages of history became increasingly interconnected at every level of economic, social, and personal contact. The result is that we are now living in an interdependent global economy and emergent world society in which everything is related to everything else. Companies in Silicon Valley are directly affected by a decision in Tokyo. Recessions in other countries send 30,000 Irish workers streaming back to welfare rolls at home. When foreign employees are driven from their homes during an Iraqi invasion of Kuwait, the tragedy also devastates relatives and countrymen in distant homelands. A campaign to save trees that is championed by industrial nations creates an uproar in developing countries from the Amazon valley to the primeval forests of South Asia.

National economies are no longer clearly definable units but a jumble of interlinked domestic and foreign operations, business alliances, transnational marketing and production, and global electronic markets, like Galileo in chemicals, Sabre in airlines, and Amadeus in banking. International corporations are so embedded in foreign countries, so involved with foreign companies, and so horizontally integrated that they are true world organizations, in which everything from raw materials to parts, labor, and management loses its nationality. In an effort to "buy American," the town of Greece, New York, voted in 1992 against buying a Komatsu dirt excavator in favor of an American-made machine. But it turned out the Komatsu was manufactured in the United States and the John Deere model proposed as an alternative was made in Japan.[20]

Knowledge is the driving force in fast-moving economies. With computers and far-flung communications networks, sprawling technologies, vast information systems, and manufacturing operations are all merged in a way that was impossible during the industrial age. What is an engine block that is designed by a computer and machined by a robot? Manufacturing or information? Capital movements have been revolutionized by globe-circling electronic networks. Even the value of labor, that durable if controversial centerpiece of industrial theory, has been redefined. In the age of high technology, the nature of work changes; the ratio of labor to productivity and profits is altered significantly.

With powerful information networks and fast transportation, corporations become highly mobile. Production, distribution, and management move easily from place to place. Jobs are exported all over the world as quickly as flipping a switch. Citicorp moved gigabytes of back-office work to the Dakotas, and American insurance companies shifted the processing of claims to centers in Ireland. Britain's Cable and Wireless uses an ingenious imaging reduction system to compress and relay masses of documents back and forth between the United States and a processing office in Jamaica. As communications technology advanced, American companies became even more internationalized. In addition to exporting goods and services, they began transferring production as well as research and development to overseas locations, interacting and then merging with foreign companies across a wide front of common competitive interests and on a global playing field.

Markets are no longer places; they don't count ships in Rotterdam anymore, only the blips on a CRT screen. Production capitals are disappearing; what is Detroit when a modern car is an international convention of ideas, parts, and labor? Even the definition of a company can be confusing. Reebok is a several-billion-dollar firm, but it owns no plants or stores; it booms along on the basis of concept, design, and an incredible communications system that allows it to act quickly on market trends and to decentralize production anywhere in the world. Indeed, communications technology has been more significant than products in some of the most important recent advances in industry. The shifts to "hub-and-spoke" operations in the airlines, for example, and to "just-in-time" production systems in the auto industry did not involve new airplanes or new car parts. "None of that is different," says Unisys Vice President Everett M. Ehrlich. "What changes is the information, and that is the point—that information is now the dynamic factor of production in the world economy."[21]

By the late 1980s, more than half of all exports of U.S. multinational firms were from operations outside the United States.[22] Some 40 percent of IBM's employees were foreign. Whirlpool had more than 43,000 employees in forty-five countries, most of them non-Americans. Eleven percent of the industrial work force in Northern Ireland was employed by U.S. corporations. More than 100,000 workers in Singapore were on American payrolls. AT&T, RCA, and Texas Instruments were among the largest exporters out of Taiwan.[23] At the same time, foreign corporations were invading the United States. By 1990, foreign-owned companies employed 3 million Americans or roughly 10 percent of our manufacturing workers and, in fact, created more jobs in 1989 than American manufacturers did. This intermingling of global operations has advanced so far that a major feature of international trade is the trade carried on *within* these companies rather than between countries in the time-honored way.

A French think tank argues that the world is on the verge of becoming a "global networked society,"[24] and Susan Strange of the European University Institute in Florence goes even further. In a brilliant analysis of the international scene, she says that what has emerged is nothing less than an "international business civilization," in which great corporations act like governments and states lose authority, in which the name of the game is control not of territory but of world market shares, and in which statesmen must listen to public opinion and answer consumer demands for better living standards in order to hold power.[25]

All of this involves wrenching social as well as economic change, for the long-settled patterns set by the Industrial Revolution are being torn away and replaced by the still unformed and unfamiliar patterns of the electronic age. The extension of the mass socialization process from national populations to the world community has produced a sudden shrinking of social distance that involves a traumatic mixing of cultures. Human interactions, more personally felt and on a larger scale than was possible even a few decades ago, are breaking down old ideological walls, challenging old myths but also creating new ones, correcting some stereotypes but reinforcing others, so that we are confronted with a series of paradoxes. Better understanding of other societies promotes comity in one way but increases frictions in another. In the very act of drawing people closer together, modern communications destroy the cultural isolation in which misunderstanding ferments but, often at the same time, intensifies perceptions of difference that increase social antagonisms and promote social fragmentation.

Millions of foreign workers and managers, for example, become much more acutely aware of similarities and differences when they are thrown into close working relationships. Americans working for Japanese companies learn in the intimacy of the employer-employee relationship how the Japanese do things; they develop their own impressions, likes, and dislikes. In one remarkable episode, American employees cheered and chanted, "One Team, One Team!"

at the Nissan auto plant in Smyrna, Tennessee. They had just given their bosses a vote of confidence by rejecting the United Auto Workers union after an eighteen-month organizing campaign. Japanese managers were credited with improving worker productivity at companies like Firestone and at a troubled GM plant in Fremont, California, where Toyota joined GM in a joint venture.[26] But there also have been many cultural collisions, mostly centering on charges by workers and executives of an anti-American bias in the closed world of Japanese management. "Non-Americans run important divisions of major American-based multinationals," says James Fallows, a well-known observer and critic of Japan. "Japanese citizens run virtually all important divisions of major Japanese firms."[27]

On the other side of the world, meanwhile, thousands of Chinese workers are also working under Japanese managers and copying Japanese methods. This, in a country that only five decades earlier had been suffering under a brutal Japanese military occupation. Likewise, German managers and Turkish "guest workers" or French technicians and Malian employees learn each other's ways and naturally find that life-styles clash. Some 40 percent of new employees at a McDonald's in Yugoslavia quit at one point because the work involved too much pressure. A woman in Russia told a reporter she did not want to work like an American; the good thing about her country was that "if you don't want to work hard, you don't have to."[28]

In a way, the global intermingling of societies is analogous to the urbanization of national societies. As more and more millions are compressed into smaller cells of life in cities, stacked on shelves inside ever higher buildings, the telltale signs of urbanization appear: congestion, personal conflicts, social tensions, crime, and constant breakdowns in civic services and infrastructure. Now mass communications and fast transportation have brought the whole world into the range of these urbanlike forces. The stresses of social density are felt far beyond cities and nations. So there is no contradiction in the fact that the present great shift of history toward an interconnected world should also be marked by a global—or nearly global—epidemic of tribal conflicts and international frictions.

"We should recognize," says Sony's famous chairman, Akio Morita, "that friction seldom occurs with those who are far from you. Friction occurs as we move closer."[29] And this is what television does so well: it moves us closer to other people by bringing them into our living rooms. Scenes of police clubbing blacks not only inflamed antiapartheid protesters in South Africa but triggered demonstrations in the United States, Europe, and elsewhere. When Soviet television broadcast dramatic pictures of Soviet troops crushing warring Armenians and Azerbaijanis in Baku, including a graphic simulation of blood running down the TV screen, it produced such a violent public backlash that the military was forced to rescind a call-up of reservists. When rioters raged through south-central Los Angeles in 1992, attacking Koreans and burning and looting their stores, protests immediately followed in South Korea, where the government had to order special security forces into action to protect Americans. And within hours Korea's best-known opposition leader, Kim Dae Jung, was in Los Angeles touring the ruins and an official government delegation was meeting with Mayor Tom Bradley.

The "friction of inescapable interdependence," as Morita puts it, is demonstrated in a spectacular way by the collision of emotions between Americans and Japanese. Seemingly standard economic differences ballooned into angry exchanges, evoking ethnic stereotypes and exposing socioracial biases that deeply scarred relations between the two economic superpowers. It was as if the old wartime animosities that General Douglas MacArthur had locked away in an occupation vault had been released and recirculated by newspapers and television to new generations. With the full cooperation of the mass media in both countries, Japan bashing—*Nihon Tataki* in a newly coined phrase—became a major industry in the United States, and anti-Americanism or *Kenbei,* also a new word, rose to a roar in Japan.

Even U.S. specialists on Japan were shaken by the harshly critical book *The Japan That Can Say No* by Morita and a prominent politician, Shintaro Ishihara. In it Ishihara charges that the attack on Japan's trade practices was an act of racism like the dropping of the atomic bomb in 1945. "American racial prejudice," he says, "is based upon the cultural belief that the modern era is the creation of the white race, including Americans."[30] By the time President Bush made his pathetic job-hunting trip to Tokyo in 1992, U.S.-Japanese relations were a shambles. Prime Minister Kiichi Miyazawa talked about Americans lacking "a work ethic," and the speaker of the lower house of Parliament, Yoshio Sakurauchi, said American workers were "lazy" and a third were illiterate. To close the circle, Sen. Ernest F. Hollings then told American workers to draw a picture of a "mushroom cloud" and label it "Made in America by lazy and illiterate Americans and tested in Japan."[31] Mass opinion had hardened into mass emotionalized stereotypes that ran roughshod through the economies and politics of both countries.

The condensation of global life that intensifies friction between countries also attacks their isolation. And this is another extraordinary consequence of the integrating forces of the electronic age. Great civilizations, locked for centuries in their individual spheres, are being driven into the maelstrom of the modern world, forced to mingle and interact with other societies and adjust to other cultures in a single global economic system. Old divisions between East and West blur in the general rush to market economies. Nations that once fought against any kind of alien penetration are now eagerly soaking up ideas and technologies from all over the planet. From South Korea to Indonesia, Asians are quick to use, reject, or improve Western ideas while Westerners are learning the hard way to respect their Asian competitors.

The assault of modernizing trends on isolationism is seen best, perhaps, in China, which militantly resisted foreign influences throughout its long history. Even after World War II, while science and technology convulsed the industrial world, China lay hidden in Mao's dreams, waiting for an imaginary future that never came. When I was there in 1975, the Great Proletarian Revolution was in full swing. The head of a large Shanghai high school was a "master worker" with only a fourth-grade education, and intellectuals were harvesting wheat at May 7 schools to "learn from the peasants." But when I returned to China in 1988, the whole picture had changed dramatically. Deng Xiaoping had launched his "four modernizations," thousands of Chinese were being trained in foreign universities, Western ideas were being imported by the carload, and the economy had started bounding ahead by an incredible 9 or 10 percent a year.

The swift change was not voluntary; it was forced by the avalanche of earth-circling information, technology, and transnational business operations that were creating a new global system, which China had to join or face catastrophe. Deng argued that China had to open its doors to the outside world because isolation had only landed the country "in poverty, backwardness, and ignorance." Even after the Tiananmen Square massacre Deng argued that, if anything, "our reforms and openness have not proceeded adequately enough." Without "a good flow of information," he suggested, China would be like "a man whose nose is blocked and whose ears and eyes are shut."[32] By openness, of course, Deng meant access to foreign technology, not to foreign ideologies. But he could no longer control information the way Beijing used to. People could not be locked into separate cells of knowledge, because news of the outside world was flowing into the country through a thousand channels that censors might hamper but could not really block. The isolation that had prevailed for centuries was no longer possible.

In Russia, as we have seen, television and other advances in communications and transportation broke down the isolation of regions and cultures to create a kind of national society. At the same time, isolation of the people from the outside world was being eroded, first, by uncensorable inflows of foreign news and information and, second, by a desperate reaching out for Western technology and ideas to rescue a collapsing economy. In a few brief years, the country drove boldly to enter the mainstream of the Western economic system and became intensively and extensively entwined with Western ways of working and living, more so even than in the days when Russian intellectuals preferred French to their vernacular and Peter the Great championed European technology and education as the path to modernization.

Similar trends have developed in other countries, large and small, where the pressures of global economic integration are also being felt. In Latin America, for example, the failure of economic isolation contributed to the fall of several military governments, and now elected presidents, no longer able to justify old-style nationalism, are trying to become fully accredited members of the global market.

Even more interesting, perhaps, nations like Japan and the United States, at the high end of the technological scale, are being forced to shed their isolationist tendencies.

To talk about Japan's isolation while that nation's economic engines are running full speed on five continents sounds like a contradiction in terms. But this is not the case. Japan is in the world but not yet fully of it, which is to say that its industrial powerhouse is working inside the Western economic system but its culture and politics still stand on its own closed island of civilization. It has accepted the alms of free-market capitalism without joining the congregation. Its resistance to foreign intrusions is legendary, and critics like Karel Van Wolferen are pessimistic about any breakthroughs. Nevertheless, several factors are at least working in the direction of more openness to other cultures. Peter Tarnoff, president of the Council on Foreign Relations, cited communications technology and increased travel as two reasons why young Japanese are now much more familiar with foreign cultures and think more internationally than before.[33] Another point is that the Japanese are not just foreign traders but a daily presence in other countries, where they own businesses and employ thousands of workers. Relations are people-to-people, instead of just government-to-government. Close working contacts may increase personal and social tensions, as we have seen, but they also provide a firsthand education in another country's way of life. This, at least, reduces the ignorance and cultural isolation which invite dangerous misunderstandings.

Cultural isolation is a problem for the United States as well as Japan. Despite its role in World War II and long years in the front trenches of the Cold War, it is a curiously provincial society. For everywhere Americans have traveled in the last fifty years, they have carried their civilization with them. No matter what foreign countries they have worked or fought in, they have moved almost invariably in a bubble of their own preconceptions. They have been isolated by their superiority complex and a messianic compulsion to preach rather than to listen. As a result, they seldom look inside other civilizations, to see foreigners as they see themselves or to see the United States as foreigners see it. A McDonald's on Moscow's Pushkin Square and Kojak fans in Santiago are taken for cultural victory; it therefore follows that there is no need to learn other people's ways. So cultural bias and ignorance of an alien society led the United States into Vietnam. And a different way of looking at the world contributed to colossal misjudgments in places like Iran and Lebanon.

There is no cure-all for these problems. Cultural isolation is especially stubborn when it is reinforced by self-infatuation. But mass communications that illumine other societies and facilitate the sharing of experiences in the workplace and in the world generally help to break down walls. As the lives of one society are interwoven with those of another, both are less sheltered by their own delusions. The sense of cultural uniqueness can be diminished. When Americans see the Japanese outthinking, outworking, and outearning them in a dozen fields, they are rudely alerted to weaknesses in their own culture. When the Four Dragons storm into the United States with high-quality products and aggressive marketing campaigns, American executives realize they have no monopoly on business know-how. Asian students, outperforming Americans in mathematics, science, and other subjects, sound the alarm about critical failings in U.S. education. Koreans who launch a flourishing fruit stand business in New York, despite language and other handicaps, make experts wonder why they succeed while other minority businesses fail.

All these interactions, themselves reflections of an

information-driven world, are massively covered by the media. The pros and cons of American society versus other competitive societies become a matter of national discussion. Studies are launched to see what the United States can learn about consensus management from the Japanese or about codetermination from the Germans. Drives get under way to increase productivity and improve education. Americans realize they no longer hold the world franchise on the best of everything. And the Japanese, meanwhile, are worrying endlessly about themselves, searching for their national identity, trying to define their moral direction and to locate themselves in a world beyond their own civilization. New stereotypes may replace old ones and social frictions may increase, but cultural isolation is eroded.

The experience of interdependence in a rapidly spreading global economy generates societal pressures that are expressed in protectionist feelings, as in the United States and Europe, or in a form of political isolationism, such as the America First platform trumpeted by Patrick Buchanan or Islamic fundamentalism in the Middle East. But the same experience produces a more realistic appraisal of one's own society in relation to others so that fewer illusions handicap public decision making. "These days, in sharp contrast with our isolationist and self-sufficient past," says Walter Dean Burnham, "the world economy and power structure are not likely to leave us alone for 15 or 30 years."[34]

Despite widely different cultures and stages of development, societies will be increasingly entangled with one another, more and more mutually reliant. Contacts with foreign peoples and cultures will continue to multiply exponentially, along with an explosive increase in transnational relations, interlocking social and business connections, and massive flows of news, information, and data. Whole civilizations will be driven together in real time, intertwined in a more fundamental way than ever before. The shades of centuries will be raised by constant communication.

IV

The Rise of People Power

MOTION IS THE IDENTIFYING MARK of our age. Whether it is China or Papua New Guinea, Georgia or Chile, Nigeria or Ghana, people are in motion everywhere. Still attacked by despots in Burma or Iraq, often restrained by old cultural patterns, but newly conscious of their existence, of their value and their power, they are making themselves felt on a scale never seen before. Personal impressions, rising out of a maelstrom of real or vicarious experiences in a closely interconnected world, merge with other impressions to become mass views and, often, mass protests. The emotions of thousands or millions are routinely processed by the media and distributed from the lowest echelons of society to the highest, within nations, between nations, and around the globe. The result is that public opinion, long more honored in the theory of statecraft than in the practice, has become an irresistible force for change in the politics of nations and in international affairs. And popular sovereignty may at last be spreading beyond its small enclaves in the West to civilizations never touched before by the ideas of individual freedom and the right of people to rule their rulers.

Count Vergennes once warned Louis XVI that sharing

information was the first step toward sharing royal power.[1] To share information universally, through every level of society and across every border, is to share power so widely that it can no longer be wielded exclusively by kings or ruling elites. The whole thrust of modern communications is to democratize knowledge and, therefore, to democratize power. And as the lines of information converge between citizen and ruler, political authority is diffused. In democracies, leaders have to contend with the constant intrusions of instantly informed publics. In autocracies, dogma and personality cults are destroyed when the masses are infected by unauthorized facts so that these regimes finally cannot be sustained even by force.

The last three dictatorships in Western Europe—Greece, Portugal, and Spain—ended in the 1970s. During the following decade, many of the military rulers in Latin America were swept from power. Popular movements followed in South Korea, the Philippines, and even Taiwan. In Africa, economic failure and official corruption were exposed, and public opinion rose against the postcolonial ravages of one-man and one-party regimes. "Across the continent," says the human rights lawyer Makau wa Mutua, "millions are demanding freely elected legislatures, an independent judiciary and an accountable executive," from Mali and Zambia to Benin and Ivory Coast.[2] And most impressive of all, of course, was the collapse of communism.

This is not to suggest, as so many Americans seem to assume, that replicas of Jeffersonian democracy will everywhere rise where communism has fallen and where public activism has taken charge. One only needs to tour the battlegrounds of change to be reminded of the distance between democratic slogans and the cultural assimilation of democratic practice. Although the trappings of democracy may be present and accounted for, the substance of democracy remains elusive. One reason is that political freedoms do not lead in a straight line to democracy. They produce chaos more efficiently than order and only work well in societies that have the institutional equipment and experience needed to manage political bedlam. Democratic trends also tend to follow zigzag paths through history. One immediately thinks of countries like the Philippines that are republics one year and autocracies the next. So there is nothing certain about the destination of all the democracy movements and free-market enthusiasms now seen in so many areas. But we do know that public opinion will be a powerful influence in all that happens. For people are now too profusely and too widely informed, too closely connected to one another, and too able to express their feelings and demands to be denied a far more active role in their own affairs. Technology has unalterably transformed the relationship between citizen and leader, and this cannot be reversed. There are no U-turns on the road to the future.

Walter Bagehot once observed that Britain owes its greatness to the stupidity of its people, making the point that statesmen can only be great leaders if the people are sufficiently ignorant to be compliant followers.[3] When followers know as much as their rulers—or presume they do because of their cultural enrichment by television—they are less awed by their supposed betters and more aggressive about bringing their own opinions to bear on decision making. "The nearer men are to a common level of uniformity," said Tocqueville, "the less are they inclined to believe blindly in any man or any class. But they are readier to trust the mass, and public opinion becomes more and more mistress of the world."[4]

By definition, public opinion is communication, for communication is the only way any opinion can become public. In the first instance, it is an exchange among citizens—

when individuals confide their personal views to other individuals. At another stage, it is an exchange of information and opinions between citizens and their government. The slightest shift in communications technology, therefore, makes a tremendous impact on the quality of the public dialogue and, by extension, on the feasibility of one kind of government versus another. If there is little or no communication between people and government, public opinion is voiceless and rulers are able to exercise nearly absolute power. But if the communication is intense, immediate, and general—as it is now in a media-saturated country—the power of public opinion expands and popular governance becomes a practical possibility.

But what is public opinion? "The living impressions of a large number of people are to an immeasurable degree personal in each of them, and unmanageably complex in the mass," Walter Lippmann observed in his classic *Public Opinion.* "How does a simple and constant idea emerge from this complex of variables? How are those things known as the Will of the People, or the National Purpose, or Public Opinion crystallized out of such fleeting and casual imagery?" His answer was that individual opinions emerge from a sea of fictions—symbols and words in his day and, more vividly now, the images provided by television—that represent an unseen world beyond individual experience. Images are matched in the mind to existing stereotypes, related to emotional symbols, and compared to previous personal experiences so that, as Lippmann put it, "we do not first see, and then define, we define and then see."[5]

The world created in a person's imagination is an artificial world because the media cannot supply nor can any individual grasp the fullness of reality. But the responses of the individual—the opinions he forms and the actions he takes—are real. If a crowd lynches a man on the basis of misinformation, it is a case of pseudo facts, but real violence.

One way in which many individual impressions are united to form generic public opinion, according to Lippmann, is through powerful symbols that trigger common emotions, even when the original stimuli are quite different. People marching under the banner of "law and order" might individually have different specific reforms in mind but are united in the emotion aroused by the common rallying cry. The symbol becomes "the common bond of common feelings, even though those feelings were originally attached to disparate ideas," said Lippmann, and "when a coalition around the symbol has been effected, feeling flows toward conformity under the symbol rather than toward critical scrutiny of the measures."[6] The slogan "prochoice" blots out specific differences, for example, and sends thousands into the streets in a common cause. Opinion thus assumes a life of its own that transcends individual variables.

Another way in which heterogeneous views are bound together in modern societies is the constant interplay between personal perceptions and public reactions that mass communications make possible. This is a circular exchange in which the thinking of individuals is incorporated into what is reported as public opinion, and what is reported as public opinion powerfully affects the way individuals think. As Tocqueville noted, a person may not have much confidence in his own opinion or even in his neighbor's but is greatly impressed by the collective judgment of the people.[7]

In the formation of opinion in the electronic age, TV images combine with cultural stereotypes to create an amalgam of individual impressions. These are collected in polls and reported by the media. Politicians check the polls, news shows, and newspapers to decide what opinions they should have, then recycle these back to the public in sound bites filmed in a Mideast desert or Los Angeles ghetto. Journalists, who like to believe they are crusaders leading the public to ever new horizons of civic wisdom, actually spend most of their time following the public. They are paid to provide not what society needs but what people want to watch or read. They zero in on already existing popular interests and concerns because those are what will "sell" stories. And they tune out what the public presumably does not care about, from daily happenings in Peoria or Ouagadougou to long-range government policy on basic scientific research. The result is a circular paradox: public opinion influences what is communicated to the public, and what is communicated affects the opinion the public adopts, which then influences what is communicated.

Another important fact about public opinion and the electronic revolution is simply that the opinion is known. Or, more accurately, that it is far more generally known than in the past. For centuries, kings and princes, aristocrats and educated elites presumed to speak for "the people." Barbara Tuchman once remarked that no one knows much about the serfs of the Middle Ages because they could not write their own history and nobody else cared. The United States was itself founded on the principle that commoners needed to be represented by men who were better informed than they. Public opinion was what political leaders said it was. Officials could pretend they were speaking for the people without fear of contradiction because the people had no way of knowing what they thought collectively. A citizen wondering why his own sensible opinion seemed to be at odds with those of his countrymen might suspect deception on the part of a prime minister or a partisan press, but he had no way to prove it. Although he might be awash in propaganda and recognize it as such, he had little access to facts that could counteract it. Moreover, even if citizens knew their collective thoughts, they had no mechanism for expressing them.

Now, however, people are kept in continuous touch with themselves. Every twitch of the public pulse is recorded and broadcast to one and all. Individuals react in the privacy of their living rooms, but, thanks to the media, they also learn how their fellow citizens and even foreigners are responding. Reactions mingle with reactions, even though the viewers in one room do not talk to those in another. Public opinion is quickly formed, re-formed, and then formed again without intermediaries. It develops an existence of its own that political leaders can neither co-opt nor ignore. And the process moves so swiftly that the public sometimes makes up its mind about a crisis before prime ministers and presidents have had time to think, much less to decide and lead. Before generals could send flash reports to Washington, angry Israelis and viewers in the United States and other countries were reacting to TV coverage of Scud missile attacks during the Persian Gulf war. And when a diplomat returned from the Gulf to his home village in Pakistan, he was astonished to hear friends "talking knowledgeably" about the war; they had been tuned every day to CNN and had already formed their own firm views about what had happened.

The masses do not even have to be massive to be powerful. Nor do people have to wage street battles with police—or vote in great numbers for that matter—to be active. What is important is that general opinion be perceived and communicated so that those who presume to lead feel its presence and respond to its force. This opinion may be organized by special interests. It may be influenced—even led—by intellectual elites like the students and professors at Beijing University, writers in Czechoslovakia, or dissidents in Hungary. It may be suppressed by torture and massacre, as by Burma's notorious military. But it cannot be destroyed, because it is a condition of the mind, a state of knowledge. Truth or myth, what the public believes assumes its own commanding presence in the politics of advanced industrial nations and, increasingly, in other societies as well. With the "arrival of the masses," says the Italian scholar Franco Ferrarotti, all the world's actors are now present on the historical stage. "It is not the end of the world," he says. "It is not the blockage of history. It is simply a different world" in which "the common people come out of the catacombs, out of the cellars of elite history [and] request the right of historical existence."[8]

This rising of the common people is a worldwide phenomenon that is seen not only in great events like the breakup of the communist world and a rash of regional civil wars but also in the rapid spread of grass-roots movements all the way from a land preservation group in Burkina Faso to Greenpeace protests on multiple continents. This activism is a natural outgrowth of the mass socialization of nations and the mingling of civilizations discussed earlier. Hundreds of millions of people, newly aware of their individual worth and no longer willing to follow aimlessly behind fumbling leaders, are taking up their own arms against problems their governments seem chronically unable to solve.

"Grass-roots action is on the rise everywhere," says Alan B. Durning in a Worldwatch Institute study, "from Eastern Europe's industrial heartland, where fledgling environmental movements are demanding that human health no longer be sacrificed for economic growth, to the Himalayan foothills, where multitudes of Indian villagers are organized to protect and reforest barren slopes."[9] Community action groups, a familiar feature of Western democracies, have now been forming in most of the free nations of Asia, in Latin America, and in much of the Third World. Although the movement has lagged in the Middle East, it has been making surprising advances in some areas of Africa. "Where repression has not been so thorough and broad as to eliminate all space for independent organization," says Larry Diamond in a study titled *Democracy in Developing Countries*, "African peoples have joined together in a breathtaking variety of voluntary associations."[10]

In Asia, hundreds of thousands of self-help organizations are operating in India alone. Many of these have been fighting to advance ethnic, political, and economic interests or, in the case of caste-oriented groups, to oppose oppressive landlords and governments and to demand land reform, minimum wages, and other rights. Also, as Larry Diamond reports in a survey of Asian democracy, there has been since the 1970s a "particularly important" nonpartisan civil liberties movement.[11] In Brazil, there were 100,000 Christian base communities by the late 1980s and thousands of other neighborhood associations and landless peasant groups that are a constant irritant to slow-acting government bureaucracies. In China, although government-sanctioned groups dominate grass-roots initiatives, local activism is flourishing. People are pursuing their own agendas in their communities with the least possible reference to Beijing. "There is reform," explains a Chinese business executive, "but . . . it is coming from the bottom up. It's the local governments that are implementing reform, and they'll do as much as they can get away with."[12] This is in keeping with an ancient Chinese custom that combines profuse praise for the ruler, solemn pledges of submission to all decrees, and ingenious devices to avoid compliance.

Inevitably, grass-roots groups challenge the competence of governments so that citizen initiatives turn into political movements, and local actions grow into national protests. The intrusion of assertive new publics into the political system radically changes the character of government. Rule from above is undermined, and power is diffused. Even the most autocratic leaders find themselves confronted with popular demands they cannot satisfy and with political unrest they cannot control. The result is a historic shift in the relationship between citizen and state that, not surprisingly, is frequently accompanied by violence and revolution.

Modern communications powerfully promote these trends in a number of ways. The most important, perhaps, is the mass transmission of new visual experiences that condition societies for change. As we saw in the last chapter, when people see with their own eyes how much worse off they are than neighbors or foreigners, their discontent is magnified. During India's violent 1991 elections, candidates rushed campaign videos into the rural areas proclaiming their "rapport with the masses" because the lower castes were no longer satisfied to be noncitizens. "For the poor, it's changed," says the political columnist Tavleen Singh. "You go to poor villages and they have a TV set. They see for the first time how people live in Delhi. . . . They suddenly realize they have no business living this way."[13]

The poor also see something else that is changing their outlook in a profoundly significant way. They see in the living imagery of the screen what is possible as well as what is wrong in their lives. They learn from the experiences of others that human misery is not necessarily a mandate of fate, redeemable only in a later life, but something that one might be able to overcome in the present world. A new appreciation of possibility replaces an old fatalism and stirs thoughts that they too might improve their status. This is a fragile feeling, difficult to gauge. "How do you measure the amount of dignity that people accumulate?" asks the Chilean writer Ariel Dorfman. "How do you quantify the disappearance of apathy?"[14] Yet the effect is to stimulate striving for personal betterment rather than kismetian acceptance. And this is the beginning of individual and group activism.

In a similar way, modern communications also break through the personal isolation that thought control and fear create in closed societies. In Ceauşescu's Romania, says Octavian Paler of *Romania Libera,* "a person was lonelinized, exiled into his inner self, crushed as an individual. If it had not been for foreign broadcasts, we would have been asphyxiated."[15] Hearing one's own thoughts echoed by others on radio or television, says Herbert Kundler of Berlin's Free University, "tells you that you are not alone, you belong."[16] For long years in the communist world, people lived double lives: private truths were expressed only at kitchen tables and only public myths were discussed at work or social gatherings. "Gorbachev didn't come from the moon," explains one of his former colleagues. "The ideas were inside him for a long time," and this was true for ordinary Russians as well.[17] What happened with the opening up of communications, especially after glasnost, was that split minds were put back together. People saw others speaking out—at televised sessions of the Soviet parliament, for example—and decided it was safe to speak out themselves. Long-hidden feelings rushed to the surface and were quickly distributed to large audiences by mass communications, a fact that helps to explain the speed with which private views ballooned into major popular movements.

A second major function which modern communications performs in the mobilization of people power is to provide crucial linkages between groups with similar causes. Although people can organize at the village level without fax machines, they need modern technology to provide the broader regional, national, and even international connections that convert local initiatives into larger actions. These connections first of all facilitate the sharing and comparing of experiences. This process helps individual groups learn from one another but, even more important, it tells them that they are not alone, that others have the same concerns they do. Their own courage to challenge authority is reinforced by their association with a larger human movement fighting the same fight. Modern communications also make possible the large-scale networking of ideas, programs, and actions so that grass-roots associations are able to form broad alliances and greatly expand their political influence. Individuals are linked to individuals and individual groups to individual groups in spreading rings of activism. Local issues become national and sometimes global issues. Local self-help initiatives evolve into national political action. Grassroots demands rise in bewildering profusion until they discredit leaders and threaten regimes.

This was an important factor in the collapse of the communist regime in the Soviet Union. A growing individualism increasingly undermined the collectivism which had been the stern law of thought and action for more than seven decades. The central feature of the Soviet system during the Stalin years was a great formless assembly of peasants and workers tied to the goals of the state and guided solely by the unchallengeable "truths" of an infallible Communist Party. The source of all knowledge—and political control—was the nomenklatura, who ruled over the local councils and regional soviets. Just as Tammany Hall once provided the only window on a strange new world for immigrants on New York's Lower East Side, so did the party apparatchiks in Russia hold the exclusive franchise on all aspects of a citizen's education.

The cumbersome machinery depended crucially on a monopoly of information and on melting down individual identities into rote-thinking groups. But the whole system began to crack when advances in personal communications and transportation put more people into contact with one another and opened the gates to the kinds of horizontal flows of information that are essential for a civil society. In the 1960s and 1970s, long before Gorbachev took over the Kremlin, a "technocratic glasnost" wrecked the state monopoly on information and, as S. Frederick Starr has reported, a "privatized system" of communication came to embrace "large segments of the population."[18] Meanwhile, television, which had spread across the nation, delivered its messages directly to individuals in millions of homes. This completely bypassed the vast agitprop or political agitation network in which apparatchiks relayed approved information to workers during tightly controlled propaganda sessions in factories or on farm collectives. "For the first time," Ellen Mickiewicz reported in the late 1980s, "a mass public has been created, as the new electronic medium transmits its message directly to an enormous number of individuals who receive it outside the politically predictable structures of organized groups." This "created a new and mobilized public, often impatient with the tempo of domestic reform and more than ever attentive to the outside world, particularly the West." To a great extent, Professor Mickiewicz argued, television's "enormous public" was responsible for expanding the role of public opinion in Soviet decision making "virtually from the beginning of the Gorbachev leadership."[19]

The surging expansion of television and other modern communications systems shattered every effort at government control, even during the final hard-line phase of Gorbachev's stay in the Kremlin. The public was exposed to a new pluralism of information that was beyond revocation. A worldly aware people—including millions of Communist Party members who were swept along on the same public tides—could not be returned to a past that had ceased to exist.

Together with rising educational levels, urbanization, and other trends, these communications developments planted the seeds for a civil society and opened the way to politicization of the Russian public. Millions of people began turning from nonperforming state institutions to individual initiatives to solve problems. There was, as Berkeley's Gail W. Lapidus has reported, "a shift in expectations and energies from the public to the private realm and to the emergence of an intellectual and moral rationale for the increasing privatization of life."[20] At the very time that intellectuals in Moscow were "rediscovering forgotten streams of Russian reformism," Frederick Starr notes pointedly, "other Soviet citizens were unconsciously putting such ideas into practice by creating a set of economic, social and quasi-political institutions independent of state control."[21] By the end of the 1980s, tens of thousands of informal action groups were operating outside the system, attacking everything from government corruption to water pollution and nuclear power. These groups sprang up in villages and towns, but many evolved into broader fronts and national movements.

According to the Center for Political and Legal Studies and Information in Moscow, these citizen groups generally fell into three categories: popular fronts, civil associations, and political parties or partylike organizations. In 1990 the number of national fronts had grown to 140, but by the climactic year of 1991 there were many more. Some of the national fronts merged to form major political movements like the Inter-Regional Association of Democratic Organizations, which was packed with Moscow and St. Petersburg reformers. By contrast, another large collection of fronts were united in championing Russian nationalism against Western ideas of democracy and capitalism. These so-called patriotic organizations appeared in many guises, from the Pamyat Russian National-Patriotic Front and the Pamyat World Anti-Semitic and Anti-Masonic Front to the Vernost Patriotic Association of Irkutsk.

Meanwhile, some two thirds of the country's unofficial politicized groups were civil associations or clubs. "The club movement," says a Political Center report, "is based on the idea of common support for radical reforms in politics and in the economic and social spheres, for public self-government, and the restored role of the individual in political thinking." These clubs "form spontaneously, have a huge membership and are geared for political action."[22] In a third category of action associations were hundreds of so-called political parties or "proto-parties" that sprang up first in Moscow and St. Petersburg but then spread to many other areas. These groups, including a Green Party which has been riding a wave of public concern about environmental issues, have far more members than political parties and have performed such feats as blocking nuclear power plants in the Tatar Autonomous Republic and shutting down pollution-producing factories.[23]

These popular front and civic action groups made a frontal attack on the Communist Party and the whole Soviet system because they promoted the heresy of diversity and raised the specter of mass dissent. But thanks to the proliferation of personal, horizontal, and even global communications, they could not be controlled easily, and eventually not controlled at all. "Ossified official norms and institutions were thus progressively supplanted," says Lapidus, "by new forms of largely autonomous expression that responded to the preferences of consumers rather than officials."[24] Individualism became, in Starr's words, "one of the strongest currents in Soviet society."[25] The miners' strikes, mass protests, and the rallying of young people against the Kremlin coup were only the most obvious evidence of trends toward greater individual activism and pluralism that were destroying collectivism and the monolithic political system Lenin had created so many years earlier.

A third service which modern communications provide in the cause of public activism is the nearly instantaneous linking of events on a vast scale, over great expanses of distance, culture, and historical reference. This starts chain reactions in which protests in one city are swiftly followed by protests in another city or even another country. It is a political version of the well-known copycat phenomenon in which news stories about a bizarre crime or a terrorist act often seem to trigger a rash of imitations. In the Soviet Union, for example, when a drunken chauffeur crashed into a tree in the Ukrainian city of Chernigov, the trunk of the government car popped open, revealing scarce hams, sausage, and liquor. An outraged crowd wrecked the car and launched a protest that finally forced the dismissal of the local party leadership. When the story was carried by central television, it sparked a similar revolt in Volgograd, where pictures of posh apartments and vacation dachas quickly drove the party leaders out of office.

Soon exposés and party purges spread to dozens of other cities. In the same way, ideas now travel so fast and far that what happens in one country immediately affects people in another. When waves of antigovernment demonstrations swept through French-speaking Africa in 1989 and 1990, many of the young protesters reported they had been "inspired by television footage showing Eastern European crowds demonstrating against communism."[26] Similarly, the rioting that eventually toppled an autocratic president and forced other reforms in South Korea became a cue for demonstrations in China. Students made this clear when they were interviewed in May 1989, during a huge march for democracy in Beijing. "On TV," explained Ding Sheng-yan, "we often see student demonstrations in South Korea and a few years ago in the Philippines." Another student, Han Bin, made the same point: "We see other countries' people strike for democracy and freedom through many methods."[27] These students thought they could do the same thing, but, only a few days after they spoke so hopefully, troops carried out the now infamous Tiananmen Square massacre.

The massacre itself was an example of linked events starting chain reactions in distant places. In East Germany, half a globe away, a nervous Honecker government immediately endorsed the Beijing crackdown to serve as a warning to prodemocracy groups that they could expect the same fate if they continued to demonstrate. East Germans, who had seen the Tiananmen Square tragedy on television and feared action by Soviet as well as GDR troops, were extremely anxious. But in a dramatic turning point on October 9, 1989, 70,000 people marched in Leipzig, and television sent a message that would change the nation's mood: no force was used, no Soviet troops intervened. Massive demonstrations followed in Berlin, the Honecker regime quickly crumbled, and within days the Berlin Wall fell.

Romania was perhaps an even more striking example of the ability of modern communications to connect events and in the process to change both the course of the events and their outcomes. The beginning of the end for Nicolae Ceauşescu was his attempt to evict a dissident priest, the Reverend Laszlo Tokes, from his parish in Timisoara. Tokes's charges of human rights abuses against Hungarians in Transylvania had been broadcast far and wide by Hungarian television and Radio Free Europe. When Ceauşescu tried to get rid of Tokes, thousands of supporters rallied to his defense. With this, the dictator flew into a rage and, in a closed-circuit television conference with his top aides, gave the orders to fire. Here is an excerpt from his frantic and semicoherent comments:

> *Ceauşescu:*   Whoever does not obey the warning
> . . . I have ordered them to shoot. They warn you
> and if you do not obey, they shoot . . .
>
> *Comrade Coman:*   Comrade Nicolae Ceauşescu, let
> me report. The head of three columns enters
> Timisoara. They will be directed to the centrum.
> I have ordered them to fire. They are ready to
> carry out your order.

Coman, the general in charge of the Timisoara operation, did carry out his orders. Nearly one hundred demonstrators were slain, and hundreds of others were wounded.[28] But some army units in Timisoara balked at killing civilians, and Radio Free Europe flooded the airwaves with this news to encourage the rest of the army to resist Ceauşescu. When the final showdown came in Bucharest, the Securitate forces fought to the end, but the army "sided with the people," and the dictator's fate was sealed. A postmortem study by Radio Free Europe showed that its broadcasts were an important factor in the army's decision.

A fourth function of communications, in this case television, is to pass judgment on what is real—to confirm reality or even to create reality—in the minds of millions. By proclaiming what is real or unreal, television often changes the direction of history. That is why television centers are modern battlegrounds where revolutions are often won or lost. As Timothy Garton Ash has said of the cascading revolutions in 1989, "In Europe at the end of the 20th century all revolutions are telerevolutions."[29]

On November 17, during the climax of the "Velvet Revolution" in Czechoslovakia, two Prague newspapers defied censors to report a brutal attack by riot police against students as they marched peacefully down Narodni Street toward Wenceslas Square. The public was outraged, and, during swiftly moving developments over the next several days, hundreds of thousands of people poured into the streets, with Vaclav Havel and his Civic Forum forces leading the way. The revolution was clearly under way in Prague, but because of a news blackout it had not yet become a reality in the rest of the country. National television coverage was badly needed. Television journalists, angry at the censorship, held a strategy meeting in the "garages" under the central broadcasting center in Prague. They were joined by a Civic Forum official who had slipped through security disguised as a chimney sweep. The result was a revolt by journalists that forced the TV management to permit partial and then full coverage of the mass demonstrations. At last, the revolution became a national reality.

As television broadcast the truth in Czechoslovakia, it also revealed the lie in Romania. While tensions were at their peak following the Timisoara massacre, Ceauşescu began delivering a speech from the balcony of the Central Party Headquarters in Bucharest's Palace Square while a hand-picked crowd of party supporters stood ready to applaud on cue. But for perhaps the first time in his dictatorship, Ceauşescu was confronted with the raw, unrehearsed jeers of angry people. Before the censors could pull any switches on television and radio, all of Romania was treated to live coverage of the protest and the befuddled reaction of Ceauşescu and his wife, Elena. Listen to part of the tape:

> *Ceauşescu:* I want to thank the organizers of this great popular manifestation . . .

[The crowd is heard jeering, women and children shouting]

Ceauşescu: What! What! No. Hoooo! . . . What's happening? . . .

Elena: Silence! Silence!

Ceauşescu: Comrades, stay still! Comrades, comrades. Stay still . . . still . . .

Elena: Liniste, silence! . . .

Ceauşescu: Stay still in your places! This is a provocation . . .

The uncensored scenes stripped away the stage props of power and with startling suddenness revealed Ceauşescu's vulnerability to millions of Romanians. The crowds in Palace Square surged on to University Square and demonstrated through the night and into the next day. Some thirteen people died in clashes with police, and that sent thousands swarming back into Palace Square shouting: "We are the people, down with the dictator!" Defying Securitate gunfire, they stormed the party headquarters and forced Ceauşescu and his wife to flee by helicopter.

But victory still had to be certified by television. The first evidence was produced when the demonstrators held off Securitate attacks against the TV center and well-known leaders like the poet Murica Dinesco appeared on the screen shouting: "We've won! We've won!" At the time, however, victory was still in doubt because Securitate forces were counterattacking army units in a last-ditch effort to restore Ceauşescu to power. The success of the revolution only became a reality three days later, when national television broadcast the summary trial of Ceauşescu and his wife and showed pictures of their bodies after they had been executed. When the Securitate saw the bodies, they knew their cause was lost. The question of who won would be disputed later, but people knew for certain that the Ceauşescu nightmare had ended. They had seen this on television.

A fifth function of communications is the international circulation of public opinion from one group to another, from nation to nation, and from the world community to a nation. The degree to which even the most ethnocentric society and autocratic leader are now sensitive to foreign opinion is remarkable. One reason is that with electronics destroying the tools of censorship, news and information from the outside world affect public opinion inside even authoritarian societies. American public opinion, for example, played an important role in the downfall of Ferdinand Marcos in the Philippines. A second reason is that world opinion is proving to be a coercing force on issues like environmental protection and human rights. The United States and other industrial countries, for example, have been under attack for air pollution. And the sensitivity of leaders to criticism of violations of human rights can be seen even in China. It was also a restraining factor during communist rule in Eastern Europe. With the eyes of the outside world watching, dissidents felt a measure of protection when they broke laws to demonstrate for democratic freedoms.

Also enhancing the role of public opinion in world affairs is the interdependent global economy. In this free-enterprise system, where market shares are more important than military conquests, every country is extremely solicitous of its international reputation. Bad publicity that was no more than an irritant in a more compartmentalized world now can do all sorts of real economic damage. When they do not feel comfortable in one country, transnational corporations simply pick up and move to another. Without a decree or announcement, the economic system can put the squeeze on unstable or troublesome regimes. Rulers are pressured to improve their behavior, not just their propaganda. Even before their fall from power in Central Europe, many communist leaders had a curious yearning for international respectability; they did not want to be seen by the West as pariahs. Deep down, they developed one of Tocqueville's symptoms of revolutionary failure: a loss of belief in their right to rule.[30]

Although it is difficult to catch history on the run, the near pandemic of public activism may be signaling an epochal event: a general shift in the basic relationship between people and government. The standing of the individual in society, as consumer and citizen, is being raised in areas where the idea of individualism has never before existed in theory or practice. The awakening of once silent masses is radically altering political equations that have existed for centuries in many countries. The diffusion of political power diminishes the central authority of ruling elites and improves the prospects for popular sovereignty.

Popular sovereignty, which is the governing form of public opinion, is an exceedingly rare occurrence. For a variety of reasons, it never took root in the great civilizations of Asia Minor or the Far East. In the West, democracy flared briefly in ancient Greece but disappeared for more than a thousand years, only rising again in thirteenth-century Switzerland, and then in the seventeenth and eighteenth centuries, developing with dramatic force in England and its American colonies. Democratic ideas appeared later in France and spread eventually to Northern Europe, Australasia, and India. Yet even highly industrialized countries like Germany, Italy, and Japan were conspicuous holdouts until after their defeat in World War II. And to most of the rest of the world, popular rule is still a fledgling concept, felt in many ways by various nations but still too new to be fully understood or reinforced by experience.

The battle cries of freedom, sent echoing around the world by global communications, have been the battle cries of Western democracy. Shouts of "liberty," "democracy," "power to the people," and "free elections" have been heard from Warsaw to East Timor. During mass demonstrations in Rangoon, marchers carried American flags and some students recited the Gettysburg Address word for word in English.[31] The unforgettable symbol of protest in Tiananmen Square was a papier-mâché Goddess of Democracy that resembled the Statue of Liberty as it glowed under TV lights during the turbulent summer nights. But symbols are not essence; the slogans of the Beijing students and workers did not rise out of deep wells of sophisticated knowledge about liberal representative government, the "enigma of representation" in Edmund Morgan's phrase.[32] But neither was this the case in the time of Charles I, when the nobles only invented a sovereign people to bolster their own cause against a monarch who claimed a divine right to rule. The young Muscovites defending the Russian parliament building in 1991 and the demonstrators battling police in Romania's University Square in 1989 had very immediate, concrete goals: defeat a coup and oust a hated dictator. They used the language of democracy to rally support for freedom, but the larger idea of democracy was still only an abstraction. It was an imported ideal that had no counterpart in their national history or personal experience.

Nevertheless, every act was a real expression of individual freedom and public will. The popular movements now seen in Russia and in so many other new and unexpected places in the world may not be the full-grown liberal democracies of wishful thinking. Who could expect this when Western democracy took more than 400 years to develop? But these movements are the vanguards of more modern, more liberated, more open, and better informed societies. Public activism on an unprecedented scale is now promoting a wide-ranging political pluralism that helps to create the necessary conditions for popular sovereignty. Trends in Latin America, for example, tend to confirm what Tocqueville found during his memorable tour of the United States more than 160 years ago: there is a strong correlation between voluntary associations and the vitality of democracies. These citizen groups not only mobilize popular interests and check the power of government but also create habits of public participation and political awareness that make them "important instruments of democratic socialization and renewal."[33] In his discussion of democratic struggle in Africa, Larry Diamond makes a related point. "As they proliferate and mature," he says, "such groups spin a web of social pluralism that makes the consolidation of authoritarian domination increasingly difficult."[34] Although Africa is hardly a major assembly area for democracy, "national conferences" of citizens, mass demonstrations, strikes, and a great variety of other popular actions have forced major political changes. Whereas only Botswana and Senegal could be called quasi-democratic in the late 1980s, for example, a whole series of multiparty elections were held in the early 1990s. Famous leaders like Kenneth Kaunda, who had ruled Zambia for twenty-seven years, went down to defeat. And half a dozen countries adopted new constitutions or took steps to legalize opposition parties.

In Asia, Robert A. Scalapino says, even the most rigid communist regimes are doomed because of rising popular demands for real economic results instead of ideological promises. "Economic policies and the communications-information revolution combine," he observes, "to remove the instrument of isolation from the hands of the state, once an excellent technique for preserving mass faith. The society becomes more porous. . . . With information comes the ability to make comparisons, which leads to demands that cannot be met by exhortations to keep the faith."[35] He says this is true even in North Korea, where news of the outside world is now penetrating into the general population. Lucian Pye has also noted the correlation between expanding information and modernizing trends. "The most dynamically changing societies in the Third World," he reports, "are those that have had the sharpest rise in television consumption: Thailand, Taiwan, South Korea, Iran, and Nigeria."[36] Why Iran? Because the Iranian revolution was not the singular creation of Ayatollah Khomeini but an explosion of popular discontents—from the powerful mullahs and *bazaaris* to middle-class technocrats and even semiliterate peasant masses flooding into crowded cities from rural areas. A repressive monarch was replaced by a more pluralistic regime with a fractious parliamentary politics that recalled Mohammad Mosaddeq's long-ago experiment in populist government. The 1992 elections for the majlis, featuring a free-swinging press and a plethora of opposition candidates, were wildly democratic compared, for instance, with the feudal rule of America's Saudi Arabian ally.

The transition from autocratic government to political pluralism generally moves by stages rather than in the great leaps that revolutions sometimes produce, and one of the way-stops is an authoritarian-pluralist hybrid. In this, ultimate political power remains centered in a ruler or party, and political rights are restricted. But a civil society takes form alongside the government, with semiautonomous groups mobilizing popular demands for better living standards, elimination of corruption, more civil rights, and other reforms. The pattern is similar to the one that developed when Russia was on its way to becoming an integrated mass society. However much political freedoms may be restricted, the countervailing social and economic trends create a momentum for popular autonomy. Public opinion, given more freedom at the edges of power, then moves more easily to the center of power, and public activism stimulates its own spread.

In Asia, the authoritarian-pluralist model emerged in a majority of developing countries. The most spectacular examples were South Korea and Taiwan, where capitalist economies and Western consumer life-styles boomed ahead in company with political oppression under autocratic rulers. But as these trends matured, once-submissive publics began demanding the personal freedoms and political participation that other modern societies enjoyed. The old dictatorial ways of the Kuomintang in Taiwan and of South Korean strongmen like Chun Doo Hwan could not survive.

For communist holdouts like China, Vietnam, and North Korea, even the authoritarian-pluralist stage of political evolution still seemed to be a mirage in 1992. But their leaders were obviously feeling the heat of domestic and international opinion. No longer able to shield their people from the outside world, these political anachronisms were under increasing pressures to come to terms with the modern world. The "strong prospect," in Scalapino's view, is that in these states the communist model will give way, sooner rather than later, to authoritarian-pluralist political systems. In China, as he has observed, the need for change was becoming increasingly urgent "because a growing number of people . . . were receiving word of the phenomenal material success of South Korea and Taiwan as well as of the new tides in Eastern Europe."[37] Whether China, Vietnam, and North Korea will ever find their way to parliamentary democracy is uncertain, but the increasing openness and pluralism being forced on their societies are certainly creating more favorable conditions for some kind of increased popular involvement in government.

All these trends—popular uprisings, outcries against corruption, rising pluralist pressures in authoritarian regimes—are moving across an incredibly wide spectrum of cultures at the same moment in history. Whatever the country-by-country variation, a central force in all that is happening is obviously public opinion, mobilized and distributed by mass communications on an unprecedented scale. The rise in people power is having a heavier impact on political institutions than at any other time in history, not only in Western democracies but in many areas of the world where it has never existed before. Popular sovereignty, one of the greatest of all human creations, may at last be spreading to other civilizations in Asia and beyond. This is nothing less than a global political revolution.

V

Central Casting for Leaders

THE FIRES OF PEOPLE POWER now spreading through our age are playing havoc with political leaders all over the world who are finding they must now cater to the vagaries of public opinion and operate under the imperatives of television. Instead of ruling from the heights of special authority and knowledge, they must look to the masses below for support. They must operate in the open instead of the dark. They must appeal and persuade because they cannot order. It is a profound shift in the allocation of civic power, part of a worldwide political revolution that is rapidly developing along with the emerging global economy.

The very nature of modern leadership is being redefined by the new necessity of dealing with active publics rather than ruling through elites of self-proclaimed superiority. And because television and the mass media are the instruments of mass appeal—the means by which public opinion is informed and activated—they are the maypole around which statesmen must dance. Peter the Great could tour Europe incognito, but the leader of Russia today must be seen and recognized and stand on a tank in front of cameras to be an icon of action. The very essence of leadership is altered by the medium of leadership. The test of election shifts from wisdom and experience to personality and image. A leader does not merely use television; he is altered by it. It affects what he is, how he behaves, even the reality or unreality he creates. He must fit the medium to be fit to govern.

Nowhere is this process revealed more clearly than in the United States, where television—sooner than in other countries—nationalized public opinion, reduced politics to a tiny screen, and forever changed the terms of leadership. Walter Mondale formally surrendered the presidency to television in 1984 when, in a scene reminiscent of Appomattox, he gave his final press conference after losing the election to Ronald Reagan. "Modern politics today requires a mastery of television," he said as cameras rolled. "I've never really warmed up to television, and, in fairness to television, it's never warmed up to me." Why he felt he should be fair to television is a mystery, but he went on to say, "I don't believe it's possible anymore to run for president without the capacity to build confidence and communications every night. It's got to be done that way."[1]

Mondale was not just offering a loser's excuse; he was stating a simple fact, a fact resoundingly confirmed in 1988 and again in 1992, when a make-believe world of manufactured issues, staged photo opportunities, and negative TV ads almost completely preempted the elective system created two centuries ago. Now the qualities needed to win an election are unrelated to the capacity to govern, while the qualities needed to govern are irrelevant to election success. It is a process designed to produce professional campaigners and amateur presidents or, in the words of James MacGregor Burns, "one of the worst top-leadership recruitment systems in the democratic societies of the world."[2]

The emphasis is on emotions and personality, slogans instead of ideas and image instead of reality. The method is to impress rather than to reason because there is no space in a sound bite for thought and no time for the deliberative debate that was once the distinguishing mark of parliamentary rule. Nor are there any special rewards for intelligence, wisdom, or historical perspective. Nelson Rockefeller once spent two years studying the nation's problems because "the poor guy thought that you became president by having the best program."[3] Television politics may be well suited to ordinary times, when great statesmen like Churchill can be a terrible nuisance with all their energy and activism. Unfortunately, it is less well suited—in fact it can be a positive danger—in times of challenge, which call for uncommon leaders and a more deliberative electorate. Yet this is the prospect in many areas of the world as politics and television are driven more closely together by more active electorates.

What is so special about television? Why is it able to denature such venerable institutions as national elections and a presidency? Above all else, it is the fact that even in this early phase of the electronic revolution, television has become the essential instrument of public leadership—the only way in which a modern leader can interact with rapidly changing issues and events and then "reach out and touch" the millions of viewers he must influence if he is to lead. Politicians must either meet television's demands or, like Mondale, slip away into oblivion. It doesn't matter how democratic ideals may be wrenched out of their sockets; the need for visual incitement is paramount. Study and deliberation may be the tools of wisdom, but they cannot be photographed. They cannot provide the action, conflict, stars, and plot—the synthetic sensations—on which TV's children have been raised. Theater and technology are dictating new specifications of political leadership centered on entertainment and performance.

The first of these specifications is a telegenic personality.

That old sandstone bust of the Cold War Andrei Gromyko once said without a hint of humor: "My personality does not interest me." It did not interest anyone else, either, nor in his time did it matter. It matters now. It is the conjured personality on the screen—the subtle mix of facial expressions and gestures, voice and manner—that now defines a leader for the watching masses. It is the image, delivered with penetrating intensity by television, that gives birth to infant impressions that grow up to be public opinion, which either supports or repudiates a modern leader. It is also theater, scripted scenes and rehearsed lines, dramas staged on a platform overlooking the Berlin Wall or in a sultan's palace. It is the Pomp and Circumstance of summit conferences and presidents reviewing troops in Saudi Arabia or wearing battle fatigues while touring a feeding camp in Somalia.

People everywhere, it seems, need to humanize their governing myths. They define ideals by great heroes and aspirations by personal icons. Recall the "Goddess of Liberty" in Tiananmen Square. The contemporary hopes of a nation are centered not in abstractions but in a human symbol or leader. Before the electronic revolution this leader may have seemed almost mythical in his remoteness. Now he is tele-real—a televised president, prime minister, or dictator packaged for millions. He is an electronic leader in whom a nation's successes, failures, ambitions, and fears are personified for the evening news shows. To the individual citizen, he is the flesh-and-blood expression of communal identity, a visible, living stand-in for a world of otherwise repellent complexity. And whatever a leader's private reality might be, he is re-created in the image of television, for that is the medium in which he must live, like a fish in the sea.

It is unquestionably true that great leaders have always been theatrical producers as well as politicians, no less so in the days of oil lamps than in the electronic present. The ego and hunger for fame, so universally attached to the makers of history, call on all the tools of artifice and illusion to create the legends which inspire followers to follow. Mohandas Gandhi, well born, educated in England, and a lawyer, recast himself in the role of a spiritual leader of Hindu masses, a man of prayer and heroic asceticism with a mystic faith in satyagraha, or nonviolence. Abraham Lincoln, understandably reluctant to present himself as a high-paid lawyer and railroad lobbyist, which he was, campaigned as a simple backwoods rail-splitter. Theodore Roosevelt, eager to accelerate his march to fame, hired a movie crew to film his reckless charge up San Juan Hill with his Rough Riders, supposedly documenting his macho image for later days of Big Stick diplomacy.[4] Woodrow Wilson commissioned motion pictures to show himself as the star of his own newsmaking events.[5] Winston Churchill expected history to be kind to him because he wrote it himself, carefully crafting his own public persona: "We are all worms, but I do believe I am a glowworm," he explained.[6]

In Churchill's time, political theater still made heavy use of words to weave its spells. But with the coming of television, words became subordinated to all the subtle influences of visual settings and close-up imaging. Charles de Gaulle was one of the century's great speakers, an especially memorable listening experience for anyone who heard him in person, but he knew immediately he would have to change his style with the arrival of television. "Here, suddenly, was an unprecedented means of being present everywhere," he said. "Now the televiewers could see de Gaulle on the screen. . . . In order to remain faithful to my image, I would have to address them as though we were face to face, without paper and without spectacles." He had, according to Richard Nixon, "to appear animated and spontaneous enough to seize and hold attention, without compromising himself by excessive gestures and misplaced grimaces."[7] At a state dinner once, de Gaulle gave an eloquent toast that seemed to be completely spontaneous. When Nixon asked him how he did it, the general explained: "I write it down, commit it to memory, then throw the paper away. Churchill used to do the same thing, but he never admitted it."[8] Sooner than most of his fellow statesmen, de Gaulle recognized the power of television and with it marched the French public into battle like an army.

Television was only a blip on the political screen in de Gaulle's time, but it quickly became a full-scale revolution. A flood of new technology—Minicams, computers, and globe-circling satellites—vastly extended the reach and penetration of TV coverage at the same time that mass socialization and other trends were increasing the need of leaders to communicate personally with larger publics. The result of this marriage of necessity is an important fact: it is no longer statesmen who control the theater of politics but the theater which controls the statesmen. And it assigns them new roles because it is a special kind of theater, quite different from the legitimate stage or the movies, more intimate in its surveillance of personality and character, harsher in its judgment of performance, and more fickle in the celebrity it confers.

One of the most important of television's powers is its unsurpassed ability to translate life into intensely visual close-ups. In London's West End, Richard Burton's marvelous voice carried his emotions across the footlights to audiences that were not really near enough to see his almost expressionless face. On television, however, the strongest impression is intimately visual. It is a face that seems to be only inches away, closer even than the faces one sees in daily life. The camera, a merciless reporter, reveals every worry line on a president's face, his every mannerism, his body language, his gestures. The microphone catches the words he says, the voice and intonation, every slip of the tongue or error in fact. Emotions, changing moods, and personal chemistry somehow find their way onto the screen, and, out of it all, viewers make a judgment. A stream of subliminal signals leaves tiny imprints on the viewer's consciousness about the person he is watching. Just as a whole character unfolds magically in a close-up of a Meryl Streep, so a leader is created in the minds of millions by the images he leaves on television's screen.

The images of Nixon, for instance, were the heavy black eyebrows, the forced, plastic smile, the deep voice defending "slush fund" charges in his Checkers speech or promising "peace with honor" in Vietnam. He wore masks, even during a private interview I remember, but these could not blot out the cues to unease and distrust. During his famous 1960 debate with John F. Kennedy, he won on points with people who only heard him on the radio but lost among people who saw him on the screen.[9] By contrast, Ronald Reagan, the actor, always seemed to come across as the nice guy next door, in all his roles from the Gipper to president. Less well known is the fact that he helped his image by writing final versions of many of his speeches himself, reducing complex ideas to short sentences and simple parables. "Reagan knows how to write for the ear rather than the eye, a reason why so many of his speeches sound better than they read," Robert E. Denton, Jr., says. "This style, again, is best for television and increases his acceptance."[10] Whatever his intellectual shortcomings, as Arthur Schlesinger, Jr., has observed, Reagan "understood the presidency as Carter never did."[11]

In the past, personal image and style were not so important. Followers knew very little, often nothing at all, about the personalities of leaders for whom they fought and died, and admired or hated from afar. Deeds and stories of deeds were the legendary stuff of which heroes were made. But improving technology, like a zoom lens, kept moving the masses ever closer to their rulers, so that finally, with television, they could see them every day in living color. Public figures once only imagined became real faces, gestures, and voices. Out of telltale human traits, revealed with almost X-ray penetration, real-life persons emerged who either attracted or, like Dr. Fell in the quatrain, repelled. As a result, personality has now become absolutely essential to political leadership.

This can be a make-or-break factor, because television by nature is personality; it is entertainment. All of existence must be re-created in another form so that reality is twisted into new shapes, rearranged and embellished to serve the demands of drama. Fictional character or political statesman, it makes no difference. Everything must be personalized—all problems, conflicts, triumphs, and tragedies presented in story form complete with heroes and villains. The goal is not primarily to inform but to provide the Aristotelian catharsis of emotions that is the essence of art rather than knowledge. Politics, having been captured by television, must conform to TV's ways. Leaders now live or die by close-ups on the screen.

These close-ups do a number of things. First, they put a premium on performance as well as personality. Close-ups reproduce a leader in intensely visual, moving images so that he seems to be vividly real. These images instantly override impressions which have existed only in the imagination. In the case of previously unseen leaders, the new face on the screen inevitably collides with the old one, which the mind has created out of secondhand scraps of rumor or news, and the effect can be jarring.

This was demonstrated in a spectacular way in 1989 and

1990, when long-shadowy Soviet leaders were suddenly subjected to the public's stare during televised debates and election campaigns. Many of these leaders, looking like lost spelunkers stumbling into the light from a dark cave, made fools of themselves on camera while millions of Russians watched in judgment. "For the first time," said Svetlana G. Kolesnik of Moscow University, "the people saw their authorities as they actually are, and they developed a very bad opinion of them."[12] These viewers then expressed their contempt by voting many of the worst performers out of office in elections from St. Petersburg to Kiev and beyond. The same pattern developed in Eastern Europe, where, in one instance, the Czech Communist Party leader Milos Jakes was nearly ridiculed to death by a leaked videotape that exposed his clumsy incompetence even in the use of his own language.

For gifted performers and speakers, by contrast, television can be a highway to political stardom. The reformers Gavriil Popov and Sergei Stankevich became instant celebrities because of their TV appearances during meetings of the People's Congress and Supreme Soviet. Thus, in the Moscow city elections later, they campaigned as media celebrities and went on to win, Popov becoming mayor and Stankevich his deputy. Meanwhile, professional TV performers—including an anchor on the national news show *Vremya*—won elections on the strength of their TV personalities more than any civic records. In Brazil, a young unknown, Fernando Collor de Mello, swept the field in the presidential race of 1989 because he had a TV image that, as a Brazilian newspaper reported, produced a "collective mystification" of the voters.[13] He was nicknamed the "video clip" president in honor of his TV skills if not his ability to govern.[14]

If television can conjure political illusions out of image and personality, it also has the power to demystify even the greatest of public figures. For the same close-ups that create celebrity also strip away the layers of unknown that swathe leaders in mirages. The Wizard of Oz instantly lost all his powers when Toto knocked over the screen in his throne room and Dorothy and her companions could see he was only "a little old man with a bald head and a wrinkled face." Like the wizard, leaders appear larger than life only as long as they are protected by a mystique that separates them from the ordinary. Like magicians they depend on the unknown to create wonder out of what is simple. So when television exposes every move leaders make, every mistake, every titillating tidbit of private life, then wonder is lost. A president, expected somehow to stand above and apart from the madding crowd, is brought nearer to the common plain. Although many other factors may also be in play, this alone adds significantly to the difficulties of leadership. As Ward Just once remarked wistfully, the Washington novel declined because before television the city had mystery "which God knows it doesn't have now."[15]

One example of television's ability to demystify is the globe-girdling travel of Pope John Paul II. Before him for centuries, the bishops of Rome seldom ventured much beyond the walls of Vatican City. To faithful millions outside St. Peter's Square, the pope was beyond seeing or knowing. He existed only in the mists of tradition, a mystical symbol of faith who invited awe rather than the rude scrutiny of ordinary men. Mystery was part of the pope's power and a reason why John Paul was a worldwide sensation when he began his tours. But mystery was dissipated as the TV images arrived in floods, revealing in hundreds of mannerisms and actions a man with his own distinctively human personality, style, and views. People replaced mystery with pictures and developed their own vivid impressions without the guidance of myth. And as trip followed trip, repetition bred familiarity. The problem, says Franco Ferrarotti, is that "today's charismatic is co-opted by the logic of the mass media. He cannot escape their conditioning. He is transformed into a consumer good."[16]

At the other end of the spiritual spectrum, so to speak, was the demystification of communism as a competitive ideology and political force in the world. The abrupt, almost brutal exposure of Stalin and other idols of Marxism-Leninism helped mightily to tear away illusions that had been pressed on minds for more than seventy years. It is difficult now, after so much has happened so quickly, to remember how it was only a few short years ago. The Kremlin then was so shrouded in mystery that Soviet leaders were little more than names, and Sovietologists measured political power by who stood where in reviewing stands at May Day parades.

With glasnost, however, the whole Kremlin cast was put on screen, and instead of supermen they turned out to be a gaggle of ordinary characters, some bright, some incompetent, some hard-line, some reformist, but most acting like squabbling politicians rather than inspired leaders. Strong visual images cut through the protective layer of mystery; scenes in parliament showed real-life leaders feuding and fumbling, seeming to be more interested in holding power than in solving problems. Hard-liners and reformers were seen with all their strengths and failings, and were judged. Personalities were connected to the shambles that every worker and housewife already knew only too well. In the never-never land of myth, demystification is lethal. Together with systemic failure, it helped destroy the mystique of communism and doomed the Kremlin's former ways of leadership.

Not only does television rob leaders of their mystery but it also subjects their personalities to a great deal of wear and tear. Because there is nothing sexy about government agencies or abstract issues, the floodlights have to be trained on live leaders. This is especially true of a country's chief executive, who is the living symbol of national purpose and the epicenter of popular concerns. The public needs a leader it can see, feel, and perhaps even understand when all else is clutter and complexity. The leader, in turn, needs to keep in intimate and continuous contact with the public he is under pressure to satisfy. And television needs a personality to provide an animate link between the people and their government. So in a triangulation of necessity, there is a collusion between politics and entertainment that keeps a president in the spotlight all the time. He is the star in the running story of government. His own media consultants and TV news producers collaborate daily in developing the episodes of crisis and controversy that will best promote high ratings for network and leader.

A president might be delighted to see himself on the screen every night and chortle over all the clever stunts he and his handlers have invented. However, it is in the nature of television to overexpose what it favors and in the nature of TV viewers to be easily bored. The public's attention span is so short and the demand for sensations so great that the half-life even of a hit is surprisingly short. Celebrities are just another part of our throwaway culture. To be sure, there have been long runs like Johnny Carson and Bill Cosby. Some political stars—Eisenhower and Reagan also come to mind—are more enduring than others, but these are exceptions. For most personalities, the hours of sunlight are very short. Oliver North, a media sensation during the 1987 Iran-Contra hearings, disappeared from the screen almost as quickly as he arrived. Norman Schwarzkopf, hero of Gulf war briefings, was out of sight and out of mind even before his memoirs were published. Mikhail Gorbachev, the darling of Western anchors and statesmen, was gone from the screen only days after Boris Yeltsin took his stage away from him. Presidents of the United States hold the limelight longer than many celebrities because of their four-year job guarantee, but they can still be burned by overexposure. During the Gulf war, the spotlight put George Bush at the top of the charts while also blacking out problems at home. But he later sank in the polls when the same television that had portrayed him as a man of decision dramatized his failure to act decisively in an economic recession.

Overexposure during the Iranian hostage crisis helped Jimmy Carter win the Democratic presidential primaries in 1980. The networks were covering the story like carpet bombers, and the White House was working aggressively to keep the president in front of the cameras. The plot was to show Carter looking very presidential in a national crisis and distract voters from his chief rival, Sen. Edward M. Kennedy. The strategy backfired, however, because it made the crisis seem larger than it was and Carter's failure to free the hostages more bleakly apparent. The political damage helped to defeat him when he confronted Ronald Reagan in November.

In a different way, Mikhail Gorbachev's standing as a leader was also damaged by overexposure. Among his own countrymen, he never was a TV hit. Because he could command the airwaves, he did pretty much what he wanted, delivering rambling harangues, sometimes an hour or more long, that would destroy the sanity of a Western producer. There was often a hectoring tone that also turned viewers off, and, an interesting insight reported by Ellen Mickiewicz, he often betrayed a shaky command of Russian, which was once parodied in a Moscow play.[17] In the Western world, however, Gorbachev was a star.

When he hit the networks in the late 1980s, he stunned

everyone with his perestroika and glasnost but also and more emphatically with a glad-handing style that made him look more like a Western politician than a Kremlin autocrat. As he traveled to summits with his telegenic wife, Raisa, and plunged into crowds abroad and at home, he was a popular sensation. With everything he did and said edited into crisp sound bites and fast-cut visuals, he seemed fresh and interesting. But television consumes what it uses. Eventually, Gorbachev's ratings plummeted, mostly because he failed to deliver on his campaign promises, but also for another reason: the excitement of a new personality and leadership style had been replaced by familiarity. Media overkill, incessant visual and emotional concentration on a single leader, magnifies flaws as well as talents and not only creates but destroys illusions. Even before the 1991 coup, Gorbachev's star had fallen at home and was in decline abroad.

Because television is now the life and death of political leaders, they have an obsessive interest in controlling it. Dictators or elected presidents, they are united in the belief that they should be seen by the people in only the most heroic possible poses. Their fates should not be submitted to the whims of history or, worse, to reporters and TV producers who never seem to understand them. Far better to manufacture their own visions of charismatic leadership and noble accomplishment. This entirely natural feeling is reinforced by two imperatives of modern-age leadership: the absolute necessity of directly contacting and influencing active mass publics and the need to make sophisticated use of the communications technology that is now the only practical way to reach those publics.

As a result, ward heelers and doorbell ringers have been replaced by a whole industry of politics that has grown so large it should get its own listing in Fortune 500 surveys. Media handlers, pollsters, and assorted other specialists have been breeding faster than lawyers—if that is possible—and now dominate politics in the United States, flourishing even in recessions. They also have been making brisk inroads into other countries, where there may be shortages of bread but there is a positive glut of new politics. Clients have ranged across the political waterfront from Egypt's Anwar Sadat and Israel's Shimon Peres to the Sandinistas in Nicaragua and Corazon Aquino in the Philippines.

The political hustlers, bristling with expertise to impress untutored employers, produce politics like cars or TV sets. For high retainers, they create news events to order, supply controversies for any and all talk shows, and generally re-arrange reality to suit the needs of their clients. They teach acting, including body language and sound-bite speech. Negative ads, trumped-up charges, and twisted quotations are all just part of a day's work. Although public policy is considered too unphotogenic to be important, this too is supplied when absolutely necessary.

The message to American presidents and foreign leaders is the same: the only way to get elected and then stay in power is to submit completely to TV's way of life. Every public appearance, every statement, every visual prop, every TV ad has to be manipulated to win visibility and attract viewers. Control the pictures and you control the story. Don't let someone like Reagan get away from his script. That is why the anthology of unrehearsed Reagan comments is a collection of shouted three-word answers to shouted questions during helicopter takeoffs from the south lawn of the White House. The story lines of the president must be planned in detail. To show patriotism, stand on a Normandy beach with Walter Cronkite. To show calm control during a crisis, ride a golf cart in Kennebunkport or take time out to attend the theater in the middle of a war. To prove you are not a wimp, attack Dan Rather on nationwide television. To be a statesman, be filmed at summits, at the demilitarized zone in Korea, and at the walls in China and Berlin. To prove concern about unemployment, fly a gaggle of auto executives to Tokyo with you to confront the Japanese. To show belated concern for inner-city problems, tour riot-torn southcentral Los Angeles. To prove a new generation is taking over rap with stars on the saxophone and jog along the Washington Mall. If all the political motion leaves little time for thought, no matter; it is the media persona that counts. Reflecting on one of Bush's amiable ambles abroad, the White House manager of political mirage, Robert M. Teeter, summed up: "The single most important thing is that people like his style. He acts friendly, but he doesn't demean the office in any way. He feels comfortable being president."[18] Apparently, that is all that matters.

If these trends in American politics were only the parochial experience of an exceptional political system, they might not be so significant. In fact, however, they have global implications because much that has happened in the United States, and is still happening here, stems directly from communications technologies that are spreading to many other nations. These technologies have their own agendas. They change what they touch in similar ways, even in the presence of widely different cultures. Leaders performing on an electronic stage act the same way no matter what country they come from. John Major, for example, disguised himself as an international mover and shaker and staged a mission to Moscow in 1991 not because he had anything particular to do there but because he had to show he was not Margaret Thatcher's shadow. Words were not enough; he had to have action photographs to demonstrate his political independence.

The fact that the U.S. experience is anything but unique can be seen most clearly in the panorama of British politics, which television has transformed in the last few decades, most especially during the Thatcher years. Media handlers have come to be as deeply involved in running No. 10 Downing Street as they have been in running the White House.

When television first appeared in the world of statesmen, Winston Churchill grumpily dismissed it. "Why do we need this peepshow?" he asked when he was prime minister in 1951. He later conceded its power. He even took a screen test—a secret kept for some thirty years—but concluded gloomily that he could never master the new demon. Other British leaders were equally out of sorts with the demon and strongly defended stiff rules against TV coverage of political issues and elections. But when television extended its influence over British public opinion, and media manipulators adopted techniques pioneered in the United States, TV politics took over the kingdom. As Michael Cockerell puts it in his beautifully documented *Live from Number 10,* "with the help of highly skilled media advisers, successive prime ministers have over the years sought to deploy ever more sophisticated techniques of political persuasion and image projection on television. They have regarded their performances as crucial to their election chances."[19]

The wonder of political wonders was Margaret Thatcher, who, quite literally, was made by television. In fact, a single program was the pivotal event in her sudden rise to power. During the 1974 election campaign, she made a strong impression in TV appearances as Edward Heath's shadow environment secretary. An important unpublished reason was that she was being coached by a master TV producer, Gordon Reece. She submitted to lengthy closed-circuit rehearsals for what were supposed to be spontaneous interviews. Every nuance of performance was analyzed and shaped for TV effect. She was a good student and impressed voters and party colleagues alike. Later, when she challenged Heath for the Conservative Party leadership, he responded with a derisive "You'll lose!" On the eve of the critical vote, Mrs. Thatcher appeared on Granada TV's *World in Action* in her home with her family, brimming with down-to-earth wisdom and exuding leadership potential. Although they liked voters to think they were too cerebral for television, many Tory MPs watched her performance on TV sets in the Commons. And when the ballot was taken, to nearly everyone's astonishment, Mrs. Thatcher had beaten Heath by eleven votes. She won because of twenty swing votes, which were credited entirely to her *World in Action* showmanship.[20]

When Mrs. Thatcher became prime minister in 1979, she was more schooled in the power and techniques of television than any of her predecessors or, indeed, any of her colleagues in Parliament. More than almost anyone else, she knew its importance to political survival and worked hard to master its use. Under Reece's tutelage, she modified her voice, her hair, and her clothes "in the pursuit of a screen image that combined toughness with femininity."[21] She trained herself to use TelePrompTers and carefully keyed her actions to fit focus group studies of public moods. Saatchi & Saatchi used all the tools of modern advertising and marketing techniques to promote a favorable public image. A Conservative Party marketing director even called in behavioral psychologists to recommend the kind of backdrops that should be used for her press conferences.

Mrs. Thatcher herself cajoled, intimidated, or attacked to get her way with the BBC and ITV. She totally controlled coverage of the Falklands War, then imposed a complete news blackout for nine hours so she personally could make the victory announcement during prime time, in the middle of *News at Ten*. During a critical election challenge, she and her handlers scripted an entire Moscow summit, down to the last stunt and camera position, as a vehicle for a TV spectacular. After she had dismantled reporters on Soviet television, one journalist remarked ruefully that the interview should be used in training courses for Russian leaders.

During the 1950s television was barred from British politics. By 1987 television *was* British politics. As in the United States, TV correspondents no longer reported on the affairs of state so much as they reacted to scenes cast up on screens by political leaders and their masters of illusion. Indeed, there was something quite apt as well as instructive in the fact that one of Mrs. Thatcher's informal TV advisers was a scriptwriter for the famous TV satire of British politics, *Yes, Prime Minister.* More than that, she helped write a *Minister*-type sketch and played the part of the P.M. herself with the program's stars. As well as anything, this showed the intimate connection between TV politics and TV fiction.

In her last days before her demotion from the front bench, Mrs. Thatcher could be seen performing twice a week in the House of Commons. The Mother of Parliaments, once known only by smuggled notes and the re-creative skills of a Samuel Johnson, had been laid bare to the gaze of commoners. Television had been admitted, and, almost instantly, customs that had stood sturdily for several centuries wilted in the glare. An image adviser had warned the MPs in advance that their standing with their constituents would no longer depend on the greatness of their ideas or oratory. It would depend on other factors: 55 percent on how they looked and 38 percent on voice and body language. What they actually said would count for a mere 7 percent. The MPs, within the limits of their diverse talents, immediately responded to the advice and changed their ways. They spruced up their appearances and changed their styles. They also resorted to the most undignified devices to maneuver themselves into camera range and to put opponents at a disadvantage.

During the initial months of TV exposure, Neil Kinnock, the Labour leader, tried in front-bench sallies to provoke Mrs. Thatcher into revealing her true autocratic nature on screen. Instead, she switched off her old parliamentary personality and turned on her video persona. "She used to stand with her hands on hips and bawl at the opposition like a fishwife," said the TV commentator David Dimbleby. Now she has "completely changed her tone."[22] The former prime minister herself provided the most insightful critique during a C-SPAN interview. She said TV coverage had made the Commons more of a show than before. The members no longer give reasoned, carefully written speeches on a subject; their comments are cut short to fit TV's requirements. Also, she said, the MPs interrupt one another more frequently to prove to constituents back home that they are active and effective leaders of the realm. She said she had to change her own style, lifting her head, for example, to get full facial treatment from the cameras located high in the back of the chamber. Tony Schwartz, a noted authority on media effects, says he was surprised at Thatcher's sophisticated know-how about TV communication. "She was much more astute than most university media teachers and many radio and TV commentators," he says.[23]

In the Soviet Union, there was an oddly similar scene. When glasnost turned the TV lights on the People's Congress, the deputies looked like a school of fish suddenly changing course. As one high official reported in amusement, they all started primping, combing their hair, wearing ties and jackets, and rotating their best profiles toward the cameras. Speeches were rewritten and posturing was added for televisual effect. And the Gosteleradio executive who was editing segments for broadcast was under constant attack from delegates who didn't believe they got their fair share of the limelight.

Gorbachev, the impresario of the production, had previously taken the precaution of polishing his own acting skills. Like Mrs. Thatcher, he wanted no photo op missed in the pursuit of popularity. The leader of all the Russias had his own private coaching team in the Kremlin working full-time prowling through film clips of other world leaders in the pursuit of performance tips. Reagan, the Great Communicator, was studied exhaustively. During one session, the team ran a video of the president tossing out a snap answer to a reporter's question as he boarded his helicopter for Camp David. "Do you think reporters have to submit their questions in writing, in advance?" Gorbachev asked as he watched intently. Other Reagan appearances that had been collected from U.S. news broadcasts were flashed on the screen. Every nuance of style was analyzed, discussed, and drilled into the Soviet student. Then videos of Gorbachev's own performances were shown and picked apart by his media gurus. In one tape, he was seen in St. Petersburg, debating passersby, telling people they must work harder and drink less. The casual interplay was decreed to be good television. But other appearances revealed weaknesses: he was too wordy. He was awkward when he spoke directly into the camera or read from a script. Warned about the problems, Gorbachev promised to improve. But while he was a hit in the West, he never quite reached stardom in his homeland.[24]

In Romania, the Provisional Council of National Unity was meeting in the spring of 1990, under heavy guard in the Palace of the Grand National Assembly. It seemed incongruous, but as I watched the proceedings one day, sitting in an operalike box overlooking the horseshoe floor, I was reminded of the U.S. Senate. At first there was the familiar array of empty seats, a scattering of delegates chatting or reading newspapers, no sign of the post-Ceauşescu chaos in the country outside the chamber. Then suddenly the seats filled as seven floodlights glared and three cameras relayed the scene to the Romanian people. Speakers began denouncing the minister of internal affairs for failure to take action against police who had attacked prodemocracy demonstrators. This provided the kind of drama TV likes. More significant, however, was the quiet performance of Ion Iliescu as he presided over the session. Smiling frequently, speaking softly, letting shouters shout, he was a picture postcard of calm and self-assured leadership. Although suspiciously more authoritarian than democratic, Iliescu's performance played well on nightly television, especially in the countryside. And observers cited this as an important factor in his later landslide election as Romania's first post-Ceauşescu president.

What is remarkable in moving along television's trail through countries as different as Britain and Romania is how it leaves the same footprints for leaders to follow. In Chile, Gen. Augusto Pinochet Ugarte switches to civilian clothes in a vain bid for popularity; in Czechoslovakia Premier Ladislav Adamec changes from a three-piece suit to a black turtleneck and leather jacket to project a new image in a television appeal for national unity. Leaders like Boris Yeltsin hurry to White House Rose Garden photo sessions to certify their political importance for home audiences; publicity-hungry U.S. senators fly to stand-ups in the Arabian desert to associate themselves with bravery. And Yasir Arafat hires experts to coach him in ways to improve his TV personality and performance, practicing his English, developing a more low-key style, and cutting back on the dramatic gesturing that might help energize a crowd but fails in the intimacy of a TV screen.

The almost universal effect that television is having on political leaders, irrespective of nationality, was revealed in a surprising way—and with special clarity and poignancy—during Nelson Mandela's visit to the United States in 1990. Here was a leader who had only recently emerged into free air after half a life in prison. He had been kept in a time capsule for twenty-six years. While the world moved, he stood still; while all the excitements of the electronic age rapidly engulfed ever more multitudes beyond his cell, he was held back in time. His ways were still the old ways; he had not lived with television and therefore had not been remodeled to fit its needs. So his appearances in New York and Washington, and on Ted Koppel's *Nightline,* were like flashbacks to another period.

Although he was on television almost from start to finish, he never displayed the slightest acquaintance with accepted television styles. He was grimly formal when television said he should have been conversational; he developed carefully constructed arguments instead of tossing off clever sound bites. And he kept Koppel consistently off balance with a totally untelegenic performance. "His formality, precision, and seriousness reveal just how much we as a nation have come to regard politics as a form—a vulgar, usually boring form—of entertainment," said *The New Yorker.* "This is particularly true with respect to television, where style so famously overwhelms content."[25] Mandela was perhaps "the last major pre-television politician" in the world. His style of leadership, preserved by prison, provided a startling contrast between the past and the present and, as much as anything, dramatized the compulsory changes which television is imposing on global politics.

The reason so many leaders are moving in the same political direction is that television is a medium of mass emotions rather than reason. It touches the universal core of human nature so that it leaves similar marks wherever it is deeply present in a culture. Mass emotions being what they are, leaders find they must be more responsive to public opinion than ever before; by the same token, their need for public attention and support is much greater. One side of this coin is the manipulation of opinion by swarms of media hustlers. But the other side of the coin is the manipulation of leaders by the public. Mrs. Thatcher did not clutch a newborn calf against her elegant P.M. outfit because she loves cows, and Bill Clinton did not blow his sax on the Arsenio Hall show because he wants to be an entertainer; they were coerced by their need to win public approval through TV visuals. "While politicians try to use television to manipulate the public," says Arthur Schlesinger, "the public is using television to manipulate the politicians."[26]

In the process, as we have seen, the specifications of leadership are changed to emphasize personality over wisdom, superficial impressions over reality, and immediate action over deliberative process. Inevitably, too, the way nations govern themselves and deal with one another is also changed. A global political revolution is under way to replace the governing institutions of an era that is dying with new institutions, more suited to the electronic age that is just being born.

VI

Crisis of Governance

"MR. CHAIRMAN AND MEMBERS OF THE COMMITTEE, my
name is Nayirah, and I just came out of Kuwait. While I was
there, I saw the Iraqi soldiers come into the hospital with
guns. They took the babies out of the incubators. Took the
incubators and left the children to die on the cold floor. It
was horrifying." The girl was only fifteen, and tears welled
in her deep-set eyes, but she spoke with riveting conviction.
The Congressional Human Rights Caucus was shocked, and
President Bush, watching the testimony on CNN, said he
was outraged. A tempest of anger and revulsion spread
across the country and to other nations.

Nayirah's testimony became a rallying cry in the campaign to send American troops into war to rescue Kuwait.
Bush cited her story no fewer than ten times, telling audiences how babies had been "pulled from incubators and
scattered like firewood across the floor." As Congress de-
bated whether to give its sanction, at least seven senators
listed the atrocity as a reason for military intervention. In
the final showdown, Senate approval carried by only five
votes; a switch of just three senators could have blocked
Desert Storm. Although it cannot be proved, the decision
to go to war may have turned on the mass emotions aroused

by a single dramatic story—a story that, it later turned out, might not even have been true.

Amnesty International originally endorsed Nayirah's claims but, after an intensive postwar investigation, concluded that the mass removal of babies from incubators never happened. Then the writer John R. MacArthur sleuthed out the fact that Nayirah was actually a member of the Kuwaiti royal family. Her testimony, right or wrong, was part of a $10.5 million lobbying campaign drummed up by the Hill & Knowlton public relations firm to "emotionally motivate people" for military action. With money funneled through a front group called Citizens for a Free Kuwait, Hill & Knowlton produced refugees for congressional hearings and TV interviews. It supplied slickly crafted video news releases with prepackaged sound bites and B-rolls for TV producers who did not cover its staged events.

Craig Fuller, company president and George Bush's chief of staff when he was vice president, saw to it that all the right buttons were pushed on Capitol Hill. He also had his operatives fanning out beyond Washington, making stops at No. 10 Downing Street, the Élysée Palace, and the United Nations to fire up international support for the war cause. It was a blue-chip operation all the way, a paradigm of media hype, opinion molding, and decision making. It showed how even foreign nations can buy the tools of mass influence and bring them to bear on life-and-death decisions like war and peace. It briefly exposed the underlife of Washington, with its hidden agendas and money politics. It also illustrated the impact of the communications revolution on modern governments.

For the same forces that have created upheavals in the depths of modern societies and written new specifications for contemporary statesmen are changing the way nations are governed. Massively informed and active publics are drawn into the circle of decision making. Political power is diffused through multiple layers of influence. The capacity for initiative and leadership is reduced by competing special interests. The ability to act, to make policy and laws, is damaged because video politicians with their own fund-raising machines and direct connections to constituents can put narrow interest ahead of common welfare. Government becomes so badly fragmented that it is more qualified to create gridlock than to produce results.

The problems of TV government, or mediacracy in Kevin Phillips's coinage, spring from a series of major advances in communications technology. These have deeply affected the central institutions of power in the United States and are beginning to have a similar impact on other countries as mass communications take command of modern politics. A number of phenomena are involved: a new TV politics driven by money and special interests rather than by party loyalties, a huge industry of media manipulation, a decline in the power of journalists relative to government, the micromanagement of public opinion in the cause of fragmenting single issues, and a shift from deliberative debate to policy-making by polls and television.

As recently as the 1960s, Washington was still a small town. Policy was made in the back rooms of influence. Even though their foundations were eroding, the political parties and big power blocs like organized labor gave the appearance of being in charge. But as television moved more deeply into politics, the center of political gravity shifted. More and more, it became vital to political survival to contact voters directly through television and to track every shift in popular mood through computerized polls. Suddenly, there was a radical change in the economics and also, therefore, in the substance of the political system. Seat-of-the-pants methods were not enough; political leaders had to operate in a whole new dimension of sophistication. They had to perform on television, invent stunts to attract news coverage, and talk in sound bites. And they had to deal with a bewildering array of new techniques: audio-video targeting, cross-reference polling, coast-to-coast video teleconferencing, KU band uplinks, digital video effects, robot cameras, computer animations, and image generators.

Battalions of media puppeteers had to be hired. Television ads and video news releases had to be produced. Television time had to be paid for. The costs of being elected and staying in office rose like a cliff. By 1990, congressional races alone were costing more than $500 million, ten times the amount spent in 1974, and in 1992 the figures "soared to record levels" again. Uncounted other millions were being spent between campaigns to keep old candidates and issues alive or to promote new ones into existence. Lobbyists and political action committees operated big supply depots to meet a soaring demand for slush funds. In one six-year period, fifty-three senators—more than half the U.S. Senate—received over $900,000 apiece, and some, like Lloyd Bentsen of Texas and David Durenberger of Minnesota, cashed in for more than $2 million. Kevin Phillips notes that "a lot has been written about the corrupting influence of money on politics, yet the corrupting effect of communications technology may be even worse."[1] He need not have made the distinction, because they are one and the same. Politics, in a word, has been commercialized; it is now a vote-for-pay business.

Image-making is a full-time professional operation. Squads of media mercenaries now manufacture photo ops and sound bites every day in a frenzied struggle to win a spot on national programs or, failing that, on evening news shows in a home state. Some self-promoters are network standbys. Others rush off to the Mideast or Moscow or any other place where a stand-up might catch a news wave and get them on the tube. Nearly 200 had themselves filmed with the troops in the Persian Gulf war, and during the 1992 election campaign so many were lining up for photo ops in Moscow that Boris Yeltsin pleaded with the U.S. Embassy to slow the parade.

Congressmen also produce their own programs in their own studios on Capitol Hill and at taxpayer expense beam them by satellite to TV stations in their home districts. These self-appointed newsmakers sit on their own sets with their own stage props and answer their own questions in TV interviews conducted by their own press secretaries. The canned "news conferences" are then sent free of charge to stations which happily save the cost of independent coverage and carelessly forget to identify the source. "A congressman gets to control his own fifteen-second appearance on the evening news—all the more effective because viewers consider it straight news," reports the *Washington Journalism Review*. "And the news director gets a free clip out of Washington relating to current events—all the more effective because viewers assume it's news coverage by the station, not the transmission of a political message."[2]

The whole character of Congress has changed. Between image-making and raising money to pay for image-making, the members have little time to run the government. The old world of Sam Rayburn and Lyndon Johnson is long gone. Congressmen now are so afraid to lead they wait for the polls to tell them what to think and do. Shortly before the Cold War ended, Oregon Rep. Les AuCoin wrote a speech urging a 50 percent cut in military spending, but his media consultant rejected it with the crisp comment: "You should know you are way ahead of public opinion on this." Media criticism or a TV attack ad is an ever-present menace. "When the main question in a member's mind every time he votes is, 'What kind of a 30-second spot are they going to make out of this vote?' " says Rep. David R. Obey of Wisconsin, "then truly the ability of the political system to make complicated and tough decisions in the long-range interest of the United States is atomized."[3]

At the same time, money saps ideals and good intentions. West Virginia's Sen. Robert C. Byrd says members of Congress work harder running around "with a tin cup" than making laws. "The American people do not understand the extent to which their elected representatives are in hock to the special interests in this country," he says. "Watch how they vote when the pressure's on. And why do they vote that way? Because of the campaign contributions that they have to have if they are going to continue in public service."[4] In the ceaseless pursuit of funding for TV spots, polls, and media consultants, a congressman is so smothered by political action committees that he often cannot find his own conscience.

Influence peddling has become a major industry. Professional opinion mobilizers are now so numerous and so influential that they are a kind of fifth branch of government. The number of registered lobbyists in Washington jumped from 4,000 in 1977 to some 35,000 in 1991; political action committees, which did not even exist before 1974, now number more than 4,000. They apply political pressure with smart-bomb precision to single issues and individual politicians. They spend staggering sums to elect the senators and representatives they favor and to defeat the ones they oppose. They operate alongside elected leaders in all the centers of policy-making, strongly affecting the way issues are chosen, public opinion is mobilized, and decisions are made. They advise everyone from presidents to city councilmen. Once hired only for election campaigns, they now serve year-round on the front lines of government. They also work both sides of any street, campaigning sometimes to elect a congressman and, at other times, to defeat him, working for American clients or for foreign governments—only the fees seem to matter. Lobbyists in the pay of other governments used to carry the stigma of foreign agents and move discreetly in the back rooms of official Washington. Now, like Hill & Knowlton in the Kuwait campaign, they manipulate opinion in the mainstream of U.S. politics because that is where pressure must be applied in the media age. When Ross Perot raked Bill Clinton with charges of having paid lobbyists for foreign countries on his campaign staff, the voters didn't even seem to notice.

Japan alone spends more than $100 million a year on what the economist Pat Choate says is "the most sophisticated and successful political-economic machine in the United States."[5] It draws on the services of an incredible 1,000 lobbyists, media specialists, superlawyers, former officials, political advisers, and even ex-presidents. During one debate on restricting Japanese imports, American TV viewers saw U.S. ambassador Mike Mansfield denouncing the idea. What no one was told was that the respected former Democratic leader of the Senate had made the comment in a video news release (VNR) that had been produced by a media-manipulation firm working for Japan.[6]

Colombia laid on a major campaign to establish an image of hero rather than slacker in the drug wars. South Africa recruited nearly a score of firms to remove scars from its reputation. Before his ouster, Georgia's embattled President Zviad Gamsakhurdia paid John Adams & Associates to improve his profile and push for U.S. recognition of Georgian independence.[7] Dozens of other countries from Thailand to Brazil signed up stables of insiders to promote their political wares. And even Third World nations, in no position to pay high fees, hired professional influence peddlers because power in Washington is now so fragmented that one-stop shopping at the State Department is futile. "It is not so easy to work in this labyrinth," said former Ambassador Valeriano Ferrao of Mozambique, one of the world's poorest countries.[8] So it is that celebrities like Henry Kissinger never fade away; they live on in new incarnations as advisers to the world.

The lobbying industry itself has been transformed by an extraordinary array of electronic tools which opened the way to the narrowcasting of issues and micro-mobilization of opinion for specific causes. Special interests, from multinational corporations and political action committees to foreign governments, can rummage through the entire U.S. population with polls, focus groups, and computer analyses. Armed with computerized lists and electronic communications, they create customized bloks of opinion and aim these with pinpoint accuracy at Congress and the White House. Instead of just making smoke-room deals with committee chairmen, they brandish the views of voters selectively mobilized through different combinations of regional TV stations and cable outlets. "At any given moment the sky is carpeted with videos going back and forth," says Peter Hereford of the University of Chicago. "It's like direct mail in targeting an audience. You are able to deal with single-issue groups and target them with a tailored message."[9] So a flash alert from the American Association of Retired Persons sends tens of thousands of angry complaints flooding into congressional offices. Activists do not have to march anymore; single-issue professionals do the heavy work for them.

This ability to segment, manipulate, package, and distribute highly specialized blocs of opinion with great emotional force is a key reason for the explosion of single-issue politics that has bedeviled government in recent years. Among other things, it allows minority opinion to be so concentrated and so focused that it can override the larger needs of society. "What happens," says Sen. David L. Boren of Oklahoma, "is you have people [in Congress] trying to please little tiny narrow special interest groups because that's where the money's going to come from to finance the next campaign, and fewer and fewer people look at the big picture about what needs to be done for the interests of the nation."[10] In this way, policy-making is broken down into separate pieces of special interest that distort and fragment the entire process. "The single-issue group derives its power from being a minority and usually a very small one," Peter F. Drucker observes. "Its strength lies in its single purpose rather than in numbers. Its task is almost never to get something done. It is to stop, to prevent, to immobilize." Yet, in its intensity and effect, the single-issue effort becomes a mass movement which, in Drucker's view, has turned into "the dominant political phenomenon of the century."[11]

In addition to the lobbying industry and Congress, there is a third center of power in the struggle over the electronic tools of governance and policy-making in the United States. That is the White House. The president is absolutely dependent on these tools to win public support for himself and his programs. It is not only that television decides how he is perceived as a candidate or leader, as we saw in the last chapter, but that television is the critical link between government and the public, where his performance in office is judged every day—the one place where he must be seen, and be seen to be succeeding if, in fact, he is to have any chance of succeeding. So it is no surprise that the care, feeding, and management of television coverage is the supreme preoccupation of the president and his squadrons of political aides and media hustlers.

Except possibly for a Cuban missile crisis, it is difficult to imagine any distraction that can take a president's mind off his standing in the latest polls and what he should do next to improve his image or sell a policy. Every chief of staff who has served in the White House in recent years has been amazed, appalled, or both by the obsessive preoccupation of presidents with media manipulation at the expense of even urgent policy problems. Donald T. Regan said he was "shocked" that every move every day seemed to be designed primarily for one thing, to get Ronald Reagan on the network shows or at least on the front page of the national newspapers. John Ehrlichman estimated that Richard Nixon spent a large part of his time plotting how to "dominate the evening news." It was the same with Jimmy Carter and more recently with George Bush.

One might conclude that presidents and their aides are cowed by television and that the media must be running the government, an idea popularized by the role of the press in Watergate. But the situation is not that alarming. In fact, the same advances in TV technology that have helped congressmen and political action committees have also helped the media handlers in the White House. They exercise far more control over the images of government that the public receives than many people might suppose or than journalists themselves are happy about. The fact is that pictures and action are the lifeblood of television. News producers need to get the president on camera, and for this they depend crucially on access, which the White House generally controls. Television also needs live drama, real or pseudo events to translate the daily life of government into visual illusions of bold decisions, policy initiatives, and leadership. This requires staging, the manufacturing of news which does not occur naturally, and for this, of course, television again depends on the White House. So the White House is able to create and manage much of the news that the public receives about its government.

An example of George Bush's media factory in action was the time he decided to tell the nation about his administration's valiant actions in the war against drugs. The White House team determined that words simply would not do the job; only a gripping TV vignette could tell the story. So they created a phony drug bust. The scenario, approved by the president, called for him to raise a plastic bag of crack that had been seized in Lafayette Park, immediately across from the White House. The idea, Bush explained, was to prove that drug deals "can happen anywhere." The trouble was that drug dealers did not operate in Lafayette Park; it was too close to the White House. As a result, it was only with considerable difficulty that federal undercover agents finally lured one hapless seller into the park so that they could make a three-ounce, $2,400 buy. The whole operation was staged, but it was worth it. Just when his speech began to sag, Bush was able to look sternly into the camera and flash his bag of crack with a conspicuous "evidence" label.[12] It was as if to say, "See, I'm not kidding; here's the proof." Another example of staging was the first nationally televised celebration of the allied victory in Iraq. This was not the work of a network news division or a spontaneous outburst of mass patriotism. It was the glitzy, star-studded production of Ailes Communications, the image company headed by an old Bush mercenary, Roger Ailes. This was a synthetic happening, a staged event that boosted Bush's image as a war hero. Any honor that fell to the troops of Desert Storm was only a by-product.

Michael K. Deaver, Ronald Reagan's master of hocus-pocus, took great pride in putting his client on public stages all over the world. "I looked on this area as the creative side of my work," he has said. "You had the sense of sweep and panorama that any director must feel."[13] Or that any presidential actor must feel. Substance did not seem to be relevant. Reporters were used like fans at a pro football game, to provide background and atmosphere for a TV production being broadcast to unseen audiences. Ailes, a veteran political illusionist, boiled the basic philosophy into a single sound bite which he offered to PBS's Judy Woodruff during a postmortem on the 1988 election campaign:

> *Ailes:* Let's face it, there are three things that the media are interested in: pictures, mistakes, and attacks. That's the one sure way of getting coverage. You try to avoid as many mistakes as you can. You try to give them as many pictures as you can. And if you need coverage, you attack, and you will get coverage . . .
>
> *Woodruff:* So you're saying the notion of the candidate saying, "I want to run for president because I want to do something for this country," is crazy.

Ailes: Suicide.[14]

Suicide, perhaps, but for something else: the honest representation of government. Because to the extent that Ailes and his ever-more-numerous colleagues rearrange public reality for their clients, they tinker with democracy itself. When they control how and when a president is seen, when they are able to flood screens with political ads, they diminish the informing power of the media. Even when journalists have attacked the flimflammery of stage managers like Ailes, the attacks have failed to stick, because it was not Teflon that protected Reagan, it was pictures. Lesley Stahl learned this when she did an exposé of TV trickery during Reagan's 1984 election campaign. To her surprise, the White House reaction was "Great piece!" It turned out that the visuals CBS used for illustration had far more impact than her criticism.[15]

The fact is that journalism's control over its own reporting tools and its ability to separate illusion from reality in government has been reduced. This was conceded with painful candor by Bill Kovach, curator of the Nieman Foundation and one of the nation's most respected newspaper editors. "If there were ever any doubt that press manipulation poses a threat to the notion of a free press," he said, "that doubt should have been dispelled by the 1988 presidential campaign and the war in Iraq." He noted that, during the first crucial months of Desert Storm, the media were given a "rich diet" of military pyrotechnics and speculation but denied "access to the true dimensions of the cost and consequences of the war." The government's media-control techniques had advanced so far, he said, that they had, "to an alarming degree, taken major editing functions out of the hands of the press and placed them in the hands of an elite vested-interest corps."[16]

It was not a case of kidnapping, however, because the media are part of their own problem. The same technologies that have helped to destroy political parties and create a new kind of TV government have also revolutionized journalism by promoting television ahead of newspapers as the public's primary source of news; by increasing the media's dependence on pictures, personalities, and entertainment; by decentralizing communications technology; and by vastly expanding both the outlets and the sources of news and information.

The management of free or even semi-free nations involves a conspiracy of both journalism and government. In the television age especially, they are bound by a shared need to appeal to large audiences in a medium that demands immediacy and visual excitement. So officials and reporters interact in a strange union of collaboration and hostility. They work as partners and competitors in gauging public moods and in setting the daily menus of news. They team together to draw pictures and stage events. Government is translated into personalities; issues become conflicts between people because ideas cannot be photographed. In the case of newspapers, reporters and editors control the words that describe the work of government; there are no direct links between readers and government officials. With television, however, there are real personalities, live action, and drama. Like Judy Woodruff in the exposé of media gurus, correspondents do not stand alone; they have to compete with pictures that often tell a different story than they do, and tell it with more emotional force. Another factor is the brutal competition in television for personalities and pictures, greatly intensified in recent years by a proliferation of talk-cum-entertainment programs. This constantly forces TV producers to make common cause with media mercenaries and their clients, even at the expense of journalistic independence.

The balance of power between government and the media also has been affected by the decentralization of electronic technology. During the 1960s and early 1970s, this technology was still so cumbersome and TV program outlets so restricted that politicians were heavily dependent on the networks and a limited number of broadcast stations for access to their publics. They were at the mercy of a few producers, who decided who and what would be favored on the evening news. Candidates became front runners or forgotten names according to the vagaries of media attention. They still relied on old-fashioned press secretaries to promote their selfless service to the public. Lobbyists were in a similar fix, and the media-influence factories were still in their infancy. Later, however, as new electronic inventions came on stream and media handlers multiplied like weeds, the picture changed. Suddenly, presidents, congressmen, and lobbyists were able to turn many of television's wonders to their own advantage. Politics and government were remade for television.

On the one hand, the arrival of Minicams, video recorders, microwave relays, dish antennas, cable systems, satellites, and computers freed television from its old encumbrances. News crews, no longer immobilized by bulky equipment, were able to move faster and roam farther afield to get action pictures and live reports. And these could be delivered almost instantly from almost anywhere in the world; it no longer took hours or even days for film to make its way through long relays of couriers, motorcycles, trains, and airplanes. The whole content, tone, and immediacy of news shows changed dramatically. However, TV production also became less centralized. With satellites and cable systems, film and TV reports could be flashed easily from place to place. Individual stations could import programming directly from any number of sources; they became less dependent on network feeds and network news organizations.

Equally significant, the new technologies brought TV's power, which only large media corporations or governments had previously been able to afford, within the reach of much smaller groups and even ordinary citizens. Technology diffused and, in a sense, democratized television. It made low-cost TV cameras and video recorders so widely available that almost anyone could be his own producer. Think how often noncommercial videos—cops beating a suspect in Los Angeles or Iraqi officials stomping on helpless Kurds—now make their way onto news shows. During the civil war in Yugoslavia, Croats in New York were watching private videos of Serbs destroying Dubrovnik and Serbs were watching Belgrade TV reports on local cable outlets that most New Yorkers did not even know existed.

Technology also triggered a major expansion of outlets and airtime for news and information. It did this directly through multichannel cable systems and indirectly by increasing the ability of local TV stations to produce and expand their own news programs. As these trends spread, the near monopoly of the national networks was effectively broken. Control over what finally appeared on millions of screens shifted significantly to local TV news producers and cable outlets and opened television to a much wider spectrum of political pleaders and special interests. City councilmen, mayors, governors, cabinet members, presidential candidates, and anybody else with a plug to make or cause to plead were able to find a spot on talk shows, call-ins, or interview programs. During a fight over a proposed trade treaty with Mexico in 1991, the White House bypassed the national media, taking its campaign directly into the home districts of opposition congressmen, with Agriculture Secretary Clayton K. Yeutter doing interviews in Spanish and other cabinet officials appearing on shows with local TV anchors. If Peter Jennings could not spare a thirty-second spot, no one was automatically blacked out. There was always Larry King or Phil Donahue or a morning talk show or a segment on a local station or cable channel.

Thanks to economics that often make news more profitable than entertainment, the amount of airtime devoted to some kind of information programming has grown exponentially. These developments have the benefit of increasing public access to television, which the networks severely limit. At the same time, however, they also diffuse news programming, increase the intermingling of news and entertainment, and effectively attenuate the role of professional journalists in the reporting of government to the public.

The ultimate symbol of this new condition of media and government was the 1992 presidential election campaign, when all three candidates rushed off to TV talk shows, call-ins, teleconferences, and other electronic platforms, not to attack one another but to bypass the network anchors and the press. So Bill Clinton popped up on the Arsenio Hall show, George Bush hobnobbed with Larry King, and Ross Perot bought tons of prime-time TV for his own personal use. In fact, Perot nominated himself, privately picked his vice presidential candidate, bought a fifty-state campaign army, and ran his own media blitzes without so much as a friendly nod to the supposedly all-powerful national media. Worse, he raised the specter of a new kind of government in which TV town halls would take over the duties traditionally assigned to the Congress; the press would not be needed at all. The whole 1992 spectacle was more evidence of journalism's declining role as mediator in the system by which citizens are informed about their leaders and government. It was also a reflection, as William Galston of the University of Maryland has observed, of a profoundly important phenomenon: the decentralization of both information and political power. "People believe increasingly that they can make their own judgments, based on direct access to the primary sources of information," says Galston, an adviser to Democrats. "They don't need or want others pre-chewing their political food."[17]

The consequences of all these strands of change are far reaching. Officials are the instruments of action; special-interest groups are the manufacturers of influence; but the media play a dual role: not only are they active participants specializing in conflict enhancement, but they also are the playing field. Television is where the struggle for public influence really is waged. And it is at the intersection of new communications technologies, journalism, and politics that the problems of government performance come together with a crash. How leaders lead and policies are made, the ability of government to anticipate and to act, and the overall quality of public life are all being affected in a variety of ways.

Most important perhaps is the inherent tendency of TV politics to fragment political power rather than to create a common force for common ends. Congressmen who elect themselves have no strong allegiances to political parties, colleagues, or presidents. And presidents who also run their own nomination and election campaigns feel no special obligations to their party or the Congress. "We have in effect created a plebiscitary presidency," says James MacGregor Burns, "under which the incumbent seeks to retain power and influence policy through the direct—that is, media-dominated—relationship with the public."[18] With all hands in government operating their own direct circuits to their own publics, the horizontal lines of political accommodation are disrupted; mutual political dependence and give-and-take policy-making break down. It becomes more and more difficult to compromise individual agendas to win general agreement on actions in a common interest.

Contributing to this problem is the flood of public views that are pumped into the policy-making process by polls, the media, and special interests. These promote fragmentation by encouraging leaders to follow opinion rather than lead it. Policy-making becomes a blur of immediate reactions to constantly changing public emotions rather than a process of thoughtful deliberation and reasoned response by wise leaders. The emphasis is on immediate, visual, and often superficial issues that play well on the screen and evoke public feelings but may not be central to the deeper crises of government. Polls only skim along the surface of topics in the news, so the opinions they cite are primarily instant impressions instead of mature judgments formed by discussion and the progressive adjustment of differences.

Policy-making, therefore, is a rush-order business. The pressure, as one White House veteran lamented, is for fast responses and hard decisions—or at least the appearance of hard decisions—so that the administration is seen to be decisive and forceful, even in the presence of doubtful facts and ambiguous options. As in 1983 when the Soviets shot down Korean Air Lines flight 007, killing 269 people. Although some officials urged caution, public storm and presidential outrage took command; forgetting the affinity for bungling shared by the military of all nations, the United States assumed the downing was deliberate, and Reagan called it "murder in cold blood."[19] Only later did it turn out that the attack had been a blunder.

Making decisions by emotional reflex also invites dangerous mistakes. During Israel's invasion of Lebanon in 1982, American emotions were sent into orbit over gruesome scenes of refugee camp massacres; Reagan, deeply moved personally by what he saw on television, voiced his "outrage and revulsion." Despite Pentagon objections, he quickly ordered the U.S. Marines back into Lebanon, from which they had been hastily withdrawn only a few weeks earlier. The decision, which revealed an abysmal ignorance of Lebanese reality, committed the United States to the Phalangist side in the civil war. This led later to the truck bombing of the Marine barracks, which claimed 241 lives, and precipitated another hurried Marine withdrawal.

Television policy-making is essentially reactive, therefore, rather than prospective, specializing in fire fighting instead of fire prevention. The emphasis is on the management of crises after they have burst onto the news shows. There is no time to patrol ahead of the news, searching for the unphotogenic causes of future crises before they occur, with the novel ambition of preventing at least some of the calamities which befall us. Motion is preferred to reflection because it is more visible. So Secretary of State James A. Baker III roamed the world in his jet looking for peace, seldom finding any but producing contrails of moving images to suggest action and therefore accomplishment and letting TV vapors obscure the absence of innovative thought and vision. The emphasis is on short-term palliatives rather than long-term answers. Many issues vital to the nation's future are neglected because they cannot be photographed and dramatized. Other issues, unimportant or even invented, are whipped into a froth because they make good television.

"The dramatic military operation in Panama no doubt produced a considerable domestic political gain," observes Abraham F. Lowenthal. "Steady and predictably costly efforts to help Latin America emerge from its long depression, in turn, promised little by way of media attention or popular acclaim, and they were not undertaken." It is a case, he said, of policy-making "primarily by opinion polls."[20] For Bush, the Gulf war was visual heroic action on an even larger stage. It supercharged his personal popularity, but both Saddam Hussein and the intractable dilemmas of the Mideast, resistant to TV coverage or solution, remained. So too did the corroding American problems of poverty, education, and health-care costs. And other even less mediagenic but equally profound issues, such as basic-research spending levels, were lost in the mists of official inattention.

A related phenomenon is the way the focus of public attention and, therefore, of policy-making is affected by the bias of sensation. When the screens are filled with one highly visual crisis, all hands—officials, reporters, and public—are turned to. Other large areas of the world disappear from sight. This accords with the limited attention span of politicians, of course, but it is also related to the nature of journalists, who have a compulsive interest in some aspects of human experience and a monumental disinterest in others. By Darwinian selection, most reporters come to journalism with a predilection for the game of politics. No matter what a story is, they cover it in terms of political gains and losses, who's winning or losing. When Jimmy Carter cut off wheat shipments to the Soviet Union after it invaded Afghanistan, the key question for the media was not whether it would hurt Moscow but "how it would play . . . in the Iowa presidential caucuses later that month."[21] As a result, hundreds of reporters are forever crowding aboard some ephemeral political controversy or scandal and leaving no sentinels behind to watch for other, more serious dangers. That is why journalists are always arriving late at the front lines of history, whether it is the women's movement in the United States or a fundamentalist revolution in Iran. Why they so often hear about a savings and loan disaster or an Iran-Contra scandal after someone else has broken the news.

Public officials, for similar reasons, also regularly miss the first signals of change. Concentration on one TV conflagration similarly distracts them from other less immediate and less violent but more important problems, like the massive unemployment Bush failed to notice until he was in deep political trouble. "Whatever urgent but less-televised problem may be on the White House agenda on any given morning," says the veteran Washington insider Lloyd N. Cutler, "it is often put aside to consider and respond to the latest TV news bombshell in time for the next broadcast. In a very real sense, events that become TV lead stories now set the priorities for the policymaking agenda."[22] Policymaking in the electronic age is also complicated by the increasing mismatch between slow minds and rapid change. The sheer volume of information, the high velocity of communication, the enormous increase in human transactions create unprecedented pressures on governments to solve new problems which they do not understand with old thinking which no longer applies.

One is tempted to apply an American label to many of these communications effects because the United States is where they have appeared first and in their most spectacular form. Yet comparable tendencies also seem to develop in other countries as the electronic revolution advances and as politics, journalism, and more assertive publics are thrown together in the struggle of government. Even resistant regimes that still try to suppress opposition by controlling national TV systems are feeling the impact of liberating new technology. In Mexico, political action groups that were denied real access to major TV outlets made very effective use of videos to document vote rigging in the 1988 elections. They also capitalized on news reports from CNN and other U.S. TV outlets, which could be picked up easily in Mexico on cable or with dish antennae. These reports made it more difficult for the ruling Institutional Revolutionary Party to cover up election fraud.[23] Indian politicians, similarly frustrated by lack of access to state television during the 1991 elections, dispatched their own videos to cable systems in cities and to video parlors in thousands of villages. In Malta, when opposition parties felt they had been shortchanged by the state-controlled TV system, they bought and aired their own video pitches on Italian stations, which are widely watched on the island.[24]

The exportability of American-style media politics also was demonstrated in Eastern Europe. No sooner were the old communist regimes swept away than the media mercenaries swept in like a Normandy invasion to instruct the new free leaders in the arcane arts—and costs—of TV democracy. Applying American techniques to radically different political systems is "a lot easier than you think," says Barry French of the Sawyer/Miller Group, which has advised all kinds of politicians, from Corazon Aquino to Shimon Peres.[25] Cultures may differ, it seems, but TV politics is the same. During the Hungarian elections in 1990, American experts were omnipresent, recommending shirt colors, creating slogans, and dispensing other political wisdom. The neophyte candidates soon began to look and act like harried politicians in long-standing democracies. The thirty-second TV spots, posters, and other accoutrements of *free* politics sent costs spinning skyward, of course, so the political aspirants had to be introduced to another familiar feature of media politics: the fund-raiser. The Democratic Forum, for example, was driven to sponsoring elegant balls in a desperate effort to raise cash.

In Czechoslovakia, meanwhile, another contingent of media handlers was working the "Velvet Election" front. For Vaclav Havel's Civic Forum they produced TV spots with sophisticated spinning graphics and other special effects. They even offered such nitty-gritty suggestions as: pick a spokesperson who is young "but not too young or too pretty." At the same time, the People Against Violence party in Slovakia rejected slickness in favor of a campaign that evoked the years of anticommunist resistance. Television commercials directed by moviemakers such as Dusan Hanak favored the grainy, unsteady style of an underground video. "Candidates were interviewed on camera with a cigarette or drink in their hand," the writer Miriam Horn reported, "their rumpled hair and baggy sweaters broadcasting how different they were from the stiffly formal spokesmen of the old regime."[26] Media politics had indeed arrived.

Although TV policy-making is still a strange new presence in the world, many political leaders already recognize it as a growing reality and are trying to adjust. Brazil's colorful

President Fernando Collor de Mello, to cite one example, did not have to take any lessons from Michael Deaver; he came into office loaded with natural talent. His talent for corruption was easily matched by an extraordinary flare for TV politics. No sooner was he installed in Brasília than he flew off into the Amazon wilderness to blow up landing strips that miners and ranchers had been cutting into the endangered rain forests. It was his way of showing his devotion to environmental salvation. He was equally visual about his dedication to nuclear disarmament, flying cameramen into the remote Cachimbo Mountains in the Central Amazon to film him attacking what was identified as a secret test site for an atomic bomb. Pictures of Collor tossing a symbolic shovel of cement into the 1,000-foot hole made a far stronger statement against proliferation than dreary speeches in Rio or at the United Nations. Until corruption charges drove him from office, he was the very model of a modern media ruler.

Other leaders, with no particular affinity for political television, nevertheless grimly accept its importance. An example is France's dour President François Mitterrand, who decided he had to do something visual and spectacular to assert his leadership over George Bush in the effort to end the Yugoslav civil war. In an act of considerable courage, he flew into besieged Sarajevo and was filmed touring the city while it was still under intermittent mortar and sniper fire. If the diplomatic result was problematic, the method was not: it was pure media politics, designed more for domestic effect than international accomplishment.

The nature of government and policy-making in many other nations is also being changed by an active and, in some cases, quite aggressive journalism. Although it is the considered opinion of American reporters that they are unmatched in their militant exposure of truth, similar virtues can be found in other journalists. Reporting styles may vary: less investigative reporting in Britain, where a "half-free"[27] press is coerced by D-notices and an Official Secrets Act, a penchant for ideology and essays in France and for herd coverage in Japan. In nations with little or no history of press freedom, journalists often are more deferential to authority than their Western colleagues. Many reporters—Americans included—are also poorly trained; this was a common lament among professionals in Eastern Europe, for example. Yet more surprising than the variations are the similarities. Most reporters, even in the most remote areas of the world, define news in the same terms of exceptional events and conflict, and have the same compulsion to expose what authorities do not want exposed.

In the former Soviet Union, it was remarkable how fast muckraking reporters went into action when Gorbachev flipped on the glasnost switch. They couldn't wait, it seemed, to get into print or on television with sensational disclosures of government mismanagement and Communist Party corruption. Programs like *Fifth Wheel* broke new ground in St. Petersburg with tough exposés of everything from the problems of Afghan war veterans to nationalist uprisings in Soviet republics. In Moscow, where Kremlin controls were tighter, a creative producer, Eduard Sagalaev, nevertheless brought bold political controversy onto the screen in a pioneering program called *12th Floor,* and daring TV anchors like Alexander Lyubimov and Vladimir Molchanov constantly reported more than glasnost permitted. On his program, *Before and After Midnight,* Molchanov ran films on concentration camps and interviews with dissidents that kept him in continual hot water with authorities. Lyubimov, producer and coanchor of the highly popular program *Vzglyad,* says it was the first to put Andrei Sakharov on the screen, to expose soldiers killing protesters in Tbilisi in 1989, and to describe the Afghan war as a massacre. "We were pushing to the edges of glasnost to see what we could get away with," he says. "We were all the time on the razor's edge."[28]

Meanwhile, more than 600 "independent" newspapers, journals, and newsletters were born under the star of glasnost. While party papers declined, the upstart weekly *Argumenty i Fakty* increased its circulation from 1.5 million to 8.9 million. Freedom-hungry journalists fought for and helped pass a liberalized press law. As we saw earlier, aggressively independent newspapers like *Nezavisimaya Gazeta* and *Moscow News* played an important role in mobilizing opposition to the 1991 coup and, later, in fighting off the instinctive inclination of Yeltsin and other new leaders to suppress unfavorable reporting. A Moscow editor, Alexander Merkushev, says the press has now become "the largest opposition force" in the country, and he cites a fascinating reason: public support is so critical to a newspaper's commercial success that it cannot afford to be intimidated by political pressure.[29]

In Iran, reporters have relentlessly attacked corruption and profiteering, assailing a confidant of President Hashemi Rafsanjani, for example, for promoting a proposed Mercedes-Benz plant while the masses were still desperately poor. One of China's leading journalists, Liu Binyan, proved he did not need any lessons in investigative reporting when he produced an unusual series of exposés in the *People's Daily* before being purged in 1987. Tough investigative reporters helped bring Collor crashing down in Brazil with a drumbeat of corruption stories that produced massive public protests and finally his formal impeachment. Young magazine reporters in Japan, who did not belong to any *kisha* clubs, charged into government scandals that the big-name Tokyo newspapers had missed or ignored. In Bulgaria, a TV anchor named Kevork Kevorkian made a career of defying authorities both before and after the fall of communist strongman Todor Zhivkov in the autumn of 1989. Kevorkian's weekly program, *Every Sunday*, raked over a whole range of supposedly taboo subjects and had an audience of some 5 million.

In South Asia, journalists from different countries joined forces to combat government suppression of news. At one point, Bangladesh barred TV broadcasts of student rioting, and Sri Lanka similarly ordered complete censorship of an outbreak of ethnic violence. In both cases, and other incidents as well, film was "smuggled out" to London, then fed back to the Asiavision News Exchange. Editors from AVN's member countries quickly agreed during an audio-hookup conference to protest and raised such a public storm that the censors were forced to back down.[30]

All through Central Europe in 1991 and 1992 the frequent criticism was that the newly free journalists were being too aggressive, far too critical for the safety of toddling new governments, too reckless and too sensational in their reporting. Underground heroes like Havel have found themselves besieged by the same kind of press attacks for which they themselves were sent to prison during the communist years. In a celebrated meeting with Western journalists, Havel complained that the Czech press "understands the concept of freedom of expression only as a kind of private detective's job . . . searching for sensations" and forgetting that the other side of freedom "is represented by responsibility."[31] Hungarian leaders were so furious that they tried, vainly, to clamp legal restraints on the media. All the new postcommunist leaders also struggled to keep a tight rein on their state television networks as long as they could, officially for the good of the nation and unofficially for their own political survival.

However much these trends may vary from country to country, they are traveling in the same general direction: toward various degrees of mediacracy, in which TV politics replaces old patterns of governance, fragmented power diminishes the authority of leaders, media technologies are diffused, and instant public emotions override reflection and deliberation in the making of policy. The changes and problems we already see in the United States are unique only in their dimension, not in their essence. Mass communications, by their nature, tend to open nations, involve more elements of society in decision making, and promote a culture of policy-making that is more reactive than prospective, and more immediately responsive to popular moods than to reflection and deliberative discourse.

Just as the diffusion of information diffuses thought, the diffusion of thought diffuses power. And as power becomes more scattered, authority loses its holding ground. The American experience may not be repeated exactly, but technology will make similar demands on other societies. Governments, in the full grip of the electronic revolution, are destined to be quite different from their industrial-age predecessors.

VII

New World Disorder

THE SUN WAS JUST BEGINNING to rise on President Bush's New World Order. Iraq had been a military triumph. "By God, we've kicked the Vietnam syndrome once and for all," he said, while his popularity ratings rose to record highs. He had been recognized at last as a bold, decisive leader, a global guide to a better future. Now the vistas of an American age of peace stretched out before him, as far as his rhetoric could reach. He had every reason for satisfaction. Yet even as Bush reveled in his reveries, new pictures began arriving in the consciences of the world. Heart-wounding images of emaciated, empty-eyed children becoming lifeless bundles while clutched in their mothers' arms, dying in the cold and mud and mountain misery of Kurdistan. Nightmarish scenes of tens of thousands of men, women, and children screaming for scraps of bread, calling out for help that didn't arrive, and burying their dead. Mass humanity in the grip of mass inhumanity, thousands choosing the fear of flight to the terror of Saddam Hussein's barbarity.

With stunning swiftness, a panorama of suffering and death in distant mountains that even helicopters had trouble reaching became the intense concern of well-fed millions in other countries. In the United States and Europe, especially, there was a sense of direct responsibility. As the tragedy unfolded on television, demands for action rose like a storm. French public opinion hammered the Mitterrand government. In response, Foreign Minister Roland Dumas said the world had a "duty to intervene" to prevent gross violations of human rights. Britain's prime minister, John Major, called for establishing a safe haven inside Iraq to protect the Kurds from Saddam's army. The European Community formally endorsed the idea.

For days, Bush balked, dismissing the public clamor as "media carping" and arguing that he wasn't going to be sucked into a civil war.[1] He would stand outside the wall of nineteenth-century sovereignty. But public pressures continued to mount. *Newsweek* captured the popular mood with a biting piece headlined "Where Was George This Time?" "As Kurds were being slaughtered in Iraq," it said, "Bush was gone fishing."[2] *Time*'s Strobe Talbott was just as blunt, summarizing the administration's position as "George Bush's double cross of the Iraqi rebels."[3] Bush, the war hero, self-chosen architect of a new world order, was suddenly under attack from every side. Snowballing public opinion, propelled by emotion-laden pictures, demanded a presidential response, sovereignty be damned. Bush finally buckled. American troops were flown into northern Iraq to guard Kurds against Iraqi reprisals.

The episode was a textbook example—except there were no textbooks—of the central role that popular opinion now plays in the daily governance of nations, in the behavior of statesmen, in the making of domestic and foreign policy, indeed even in the shaping of world institutions. The mistreatment of the Kurds was an old problem, only rarely mentioned in dispatches. Normally, the 1991 tragedy would have been dismissed as quickly as similar outrages were in 1988, 1975, and earlier decades. But in 1991 the world's attention was focused as never before by television's graphic coverage; millions of complete strangers became emotionally involved. The pressure was so great that Bush's own convictions and, more important, long-standing international customs were overridden. Inch by inch, the world was pressed toward the principle that in some circumstances the protection of individual human rights must take precedence over the supposedly inviolable laws of national sovereignty.

Bush took America to war for the proclaimed purpose of defending Kuwait's sovereignty, no matter how repressive its leaders might be. He then cited the same ground—noninterference in the internal affairs of a sovereign state—for refusing to help the Iraqi Kurds and Shi'ites in a revolt that he himself had encouraged. But in the end, popular opinion ran roughshod over his conventional, if artificial, reasons. National sovereignty, in the act of being defended, had been eroded. "The head cannot be the only guide to the conduct of human affairs," said *The Economist;* "sometimes logic may lead inexorably to a conclusion that the heart knows is wrong." There were risks in following the heart in Kurdistan, it said, but "having called for action, Western public opinion should be . . . prepared to accept the costs."[4]

The Kurdish crisis will get only a footnote in history, which is notorious for its biases, but it made a number of telling points about the impact of modern mass communications on the governance of nations and the conduct of international relations. Among many other things, it illustrated the increasing limits which mobilized public opinion now places on national sovereignty. It also showed how some issues, like human rights, have been internationalized by popular movements that force their way past old conventions about nonintervention. It proved how quickly mass emotions could be aroused and compel national governments to act even, as in Bush's case, against professional advice and when action would mean breaking international rules. It demonstrated how these same emotions, moving along electronic pathways, developed simultaneously in different countries, crossed frontiers, and became a common flood that finally moved the international community. The result was that national leaders had to contend at the same time with both domestic and foreign opinion. And popular feelings bypassed creaking diplomatic machinery to operate directly on international organizations. During the crisis, moreover, Western leaders had to perform onstage, conferring with one another and acting and interacting with their constituencies in the full gaze of mankind. Ministers jetted from capital to capital and even ventured into the Anatolian redoubts of despair while cameras reported their every move for public judgment. There was no time for traditional diplomacy. Statesmen were too busy trying to catch up to their publics.

The fact is that the international system has been broken loose from its moorings by a series of remarkable developments. More than politics and armies, economics now drives the world. Markets are more valuable than territory. Information and technology are more important than commodities. Unruly publics invade the domain of diplomats and statesmen. Wisdom is less valued by leaders than media skills. Local issues become global issues, and global issues become local issues. National sovereignty, the basic unit of the international system for several hundred years, is riddled by global corporations, transnational ideas and popular movements, transfers of technology and capital, worldwide news, consumer trends, and just about everything else.

Magnifying the impact of all these developments is the sheer scale, volume, and velocity of the transactions now overloading the international system. Not only have human contacts increased exponentially with improved communications but the total impact has been compounded many times over by fast-expanding populations. The number of people in the world reached 4 billion in 1974, soared to 5.48 billion by 1992, and is headed toward an estimated 6.3 billion in 2000 and 10 billion by 2050.[5] And because of imbalances in the growth patterns, Daniel Bell predicts, "we will see demographic tidal waves sweeping the world" over the next twenty years.[6] If this were happening in earlier centuries, when only myths connected continents, the impact on international affairs might be slight or more slowly felt. As it is now, everyone is connected to everyone else, visually and emotionally through television, economically through the new global economy, and even physically through individual mobility and the mass migrations being generated by visions of a better life in some more favored land. The result is a quantum increase in the volume of public business with which the international community must cope.

Adding to the burden is the expanding number of nations, a growth that began with decolonization after World War II and picked up again recently with the breakup of the Soviet empire and fresh surges of ethnic separatism. The roll call of United Nations members increased from 51 in 1945 to 175 in 1992 and will continue to grow. Not only are these nations more numerous but they are dealing with many more issues and at more levels of public and private interest. So again there is a compounding of activity that greatly increases the volume and range of interactions. "The theme of international relations must now be studied in the context of a vast expansion of its scope," says the veteran diplomat Abba Eban. "There are many more actors in the drama, more issues to be wrestled with, more functions performed, more specialized skills mobilized . . . than in the days when diplomacy was a compact exercise in which relatively few people in a few sovereign countries dealt with a few salient problems while the masses of humankind went on their way unheeding."[7]

In addition to expanding the volume and scale of international affairs, modern communications have increased the velocity by many orders of magnitude. Only a few years ago diplomacy and trade were conducted by slow-moving cables or telexes. Now, all the world's business is conducted in an electronic time zone. As Secretary of State George P. Shultz once put it, live television "puts everybody on real time, because everyone is seeing the same thing."[8] Whole libraries of information arrive in offices in seconds. Trillions of dollars flash through the global financial system. First satellites and now thousands of miles of glass fibers, stretching across the United States and both the Atlantic and Pacific, are carrying a colossal load of international traffic at up to a billion bits per second. This kind of communication was unthinkable only a few years ago, yet it will be quickly exceeded, so fast is technology advancing. Within the decade, says the Nobelist Arno A. Penzias, a single chip will pack more power than all the civilian and military electronics used during World War II.[9] Today's hyperbole will be tomorrow's understatement.

These are more than gee-whiz facts for computer buffs; they are core elements in the emerging international system. When communications technology dramatically increases the range, volume, and velocity of global information and contacts, it changes the basic relationships between people and governments. It bends foreign relations into new forms, whether diplomats like it or not, or even understand what is happening. At least five elements are involved:

- The emergence of public opinion, together with media politics, as a powerful new force in international relations as well as national decision making. "The growth of popular interest in what used to be a specialized domain has been rapid and spectacular," says Eban. "The sheer quantity of preoccupation with international affairs reflects an explosive enlargement of interest and concern."[10]

- The ascension of global economics over national security concerns in the trends shaping a new world order as the Cold War disappears into history. The old standbys of statesmen—ideological combat and strategic military balances—have been overtaken by technological competition, market shares, consumerism, environmental threats, and a confusing array of other issues.

- The erosion of national sovereignty as international corporations, special interests, global information networks, and popular movements operate above, around, and in spite of governments that still cling to the quaint notion that nation-states should control all that takes place within their territories.

- A dramatic increase in social and political strains as new information systems outpace the adjustment rate of government institutions and, even more threatening, when developing countries fall further behind industrial leaders in the technological capacity that will define success or failure in the new century.

- The near collapse of a diplomatic tradition that believed it could exist "only in the darkness of mystery"[11] but that now must operate in the open in the company of common voters and troublemaking journalists.

These elements are so interwoven that in a way it is a distortion to consider them separately. Global communications drive the global economy, but the global economy also drives communications. Together, communications and economics multiply international contacts, and these intensify the involvement of one people with another. This involvement, in turn, promotes the intrusion of popular opinion into the formerly closed salons of foreign ministries. With the information revolution and the rise of people power, says Stanley Hoffmann, "popular demands and pressures" set much of the foreign policy agenda and make it more difficult for governments to control the process.[12] To complicate matters further, public opinion seldom appears in a simple, coherent form. Except on a monumental issue like war, the public mind is a complex mosaic of individual, business, group, sectional, and multinational views—views that are shaped around different special interests and come together in different combinations on many political levels all at the same time. And these opinion blocs—complaints, demands, protests, whatever—move through channels that now often bypass the central switchboards of national governments.

Multinational corporations, for example, do most of their own negotiating, lobby with individual ministries, parliamentary committees, and special interest groups and launch media campaigns to win the support of foreign publics. "They are no longer playing walk-on parts, auxiliaries to the real actors," says Susan Strange of the European University Institute. "They are at center stage, right up there with the governments."[13] Although they are vaguely reminiscent of the old international cartels, they function differently, achieving power not so much by collusion as by global production and marketing. Business leaders also maneuver, compete, and communicate through their own international channels; they have little in common with diplomats, who may be skilled in Cold War politics but lost at sea in disputes over ISDN standards or transnational data transfer regulations. So there is a corporate impulse—often necessity—to operate outside the usual routes of state-to-state relations.

In a similar way, special interest groups are disrupting the normal patterns of foreign affairs. When American autoworkers attack Japanese competition in the United States or Australians demonstrate against Asian immigrants, for example, the complaints are relayed by the media from public to public and then carom back against political leaders. A foreign problem is converted into a domestic problem in one country, and a domestic problem becomes a foreign problem in another. "To renew America, we meet challenges abroad as well as at home," Clinton declared in his Inaugural Address. "There is no longer a clear division between what is foreign and what is domestic. The world economy, the world environment, the world AIDS crisis, the world arms race— they affect us all."

Instead of controversies being buffered by foreign offices, they are plunged directly into the caldron of local politics. "Countries are complex combinations of mobilized groups," observes Andrew Arno of the East-West Communication Institute. "In conflicts . . . it is often more a matter of strained relations between centers of interest than whole countries."[14]

Even private groups become involved in the so-called internal affairs of other countries. The AFL-CIO provided direct help, for instance, to striking miners in Siberia, and a host of similar organizations aided democratic forces fighting communist regimes in Eastern Europe. Popular movements also routinely spill across national borders without any concern for the traditional channels of foreign affairs. From Germany to New Zealand, outside groups have freely interfered with the deployment of atomic weapons and blocked nuclear power plant construction in both open and closed societies.

Grass-roots fears have made environmental dangers a global issue which governments cannot ignore. They helped bring about the downfall of Bulgaria's hated strongman Todor Zhivkov. The Greens, originally dismissed as a fringe group in West Germany, became an important international movement. In the 1989 elections to the European Parliament, they were "the stars of the protest vote," jolting mainline parties with surprising gains in Germany, France, Britain, and Italy and nearly doubling their seats in Strasbourg.[15] A green party has been formed in Brazil to fight deforestation of the Amazon. Another green faction has sprouted in Australia's Labor Party. And similar environmental groups are active in the politics of Canada, Mexico, Japan, India, West Africa, and Central America. In fact, according to a report on "ecopolitics," the environmental movement has "spawned an increasingly influential voting bloc" in most of the world's industrial countries, with activist groups waging media campaigns, passing legislation, electing politicians, and influencing policies "internationally as well as domestically."[16]

Most impressive of all, however, is the way public opinion is pressuring governments in the struggle over human rights. An "astounding expansion of individual rights," says the political scientist Robert A. Dahl, is one of the striking features that distinguish modern democracies from their predecessors. One reason, he says, is the sheer scale of today's democracies, which requires a number of political rights that "go well beyond those that citizens were entitled to in earlier democratic and republican orders."[17] Another, more immediate reason is that highly publicized protests in one country are immediately relayed to another. Thus, pro-

test movements in South Africa or South Korea rally emotions thousands of miles away. Escalating public pressures
drive egalitarian trends across national borders and through
old ideological barriers.

When Moscow accepted the Helsinki Accords in 1975,
foreign diplomats and journalists reacted with generic cyni-
cism. They dismissed Soviet endorsement of the so-called
Basket Three principles on human rights as a hollow pledge
made only to win Western recognition of postwar frontiers.
Jimmy Carter later made human rights speeches, Congress
passed laws, and the State Department issued annual reports
that, predictably, found more rights violations among communist enemies than among friendly dictators. But the war-
riors of the Cold War did not assign much practical effect
to all the fanfare. Jeane Kirkpatrick, who was to become
Ronald Reagan's representative to the United Nations, even
accused Carter of damaging America's strategic interests
with his human rights crusading.[18]

So it came as something of a surprise to a traveler making
the rounds of Eastern Europe to hear the Helsinki Accords
often mentioned as an important factor in the serial revolts
of 1989. Germany's Christoph Royen, an authority on the
former Soviet Union and Eastern Europe, says, "many people in the West thought Helsinki was a defeat for the West.
They didn't realize—and the Russians didn't either—that
the Soviets were in a way signing their own death war-
rant."[19] Helsinki Watch committees were set up in many
countries, even the Soviet Union, despite brutal repression
and the imprisonment of such activists as Yuri Orlov. Violations were recorded and denounced by organizations like
Amnesty International. Incidents were reported around the
world by the BBC, the Voice of America, and many TV
programs that penetrated national frontiers. "The political
prominence of human rights owes a great deal . . . to postwar

changes in the means of communications," Seweryn Bialer and Michael Mandelbaum observe. "Television has made a difference. The victims of human rights violations now have faces as well as names that are broadcast around the world."[20]

While foreign ministries dragged their feet on the rights issue, citizen movements gathered force. Opinions coalesced around a belief that individual rights are universal in their validity and therefore should be universal in their application, regardless of political system. Although many nations oppose any interference in their internal affairs, these affairs are not so internal anymore; rising waves of public opinion have reached distant shores. Even Beijing revealed its sensitivity when it invited Australian human rights experts to make on-site inspections in China in an effort to soften support for post-Tiananmen sanctions.

Still more startling is the new custom of recruiting foreign observers to certify the validity of a nation's own elections, both to ratify the process for the voters themselves and to win the world's approval. In 1989, for instance, the Council of Freely Elected Heads of Government, headed by Jimmy Carter, observed firsthand and then denounced vote rigging in Manuel Noriega's Panama, setting the stage for the U.S. invasion. The following year the council's star-studded cast of ballot watchers found the Nicaraguan elections free and fair: "Voting procedures were excellent. A secret vote and honest count occurred."[21] A wobbly democracy emerged from the rubble of civil war and East-West conflict. For a number of countries, it now seems, the humiliation of foreign intervention is outweighed by the need for the approval of foreign publics and even world opinion.

An important implication is that a broad popular consensus on human rights may now be evolving to the point where it could undergird international actions to protect ethnic and national minorities against sovereign majorities. With empires like the former Soviet Union falling apart and jerry-built nations in Central Europe, Africa, and elsewhere torn by ethnic strife, outside pressure to defend individual rights may be the only way to prevent or stop civil wars. Stanley Hoffmann observed gloomily in 1983 that an effective international defense of human rights would require revolutionary changes because the whole thrust of individual human rights is "dangerously subversive" to authoritarian regimes.[22] But some of these changes became reality during the revolutionary events from 1989 through 1991. Incredibly, an international conference on human rights was held in Moscow in 1991, with the Russian representative declaring that "national guarantees are not sufficient so we have to review the principle of non-interference in affairs of other governments."[23] Despite all the cross-cultural complexities and political obstacles that bedevil civil rights questions, there is wide popular support for the primacy of individual rights over sovereign prerogatives, which formerly made nations the sole judge of the way subjects are treated.

The idea of national sovereignty has anchored the international system for centuries, or at least since thinkers like Jean Bodin and Thomas Hobbes first explored the concept. The nation-state has been the centerpiece of global politics, honored in breach as well as observance. Countries have been conquered and frontiers changed in the name of national claims. Statesmen could ignore a holocaust as long as sovereignty remained the supreme principle of world order or disorder, and the public of one country did not independently interfere with the public of another. After World War II the idea of shared sovereignty was introduced in the United Nations, as it had been earlier in the League of Nations. At the same time, the great French visionary Jean Monnet started the historic movement that eventually led to the European Community. His objective was "to make a breach in the ramparts of national sovereignty which will be narrow enough to secure consent but deep enough to open the way toward the unity that is essential to peace."[24] But the really frontal attack on national sovereignty came in the 1970s and 1980s, when the communications revolution, jet-fast travel, and related trends broke across national frontiers and started the cycle of change that led to a new, interdependent global economy. The power of the state, once sustained by monopolies of information, is now diminished by the real-time diffusion of information to whole populations. The very nature of the modern state is being redefined and the relations between nations profoundly altered.

First, there has been a major shift in the center of gravity of advanced nations from economies based on manufacturing to economies based on information and communication. Ideas, technology, data, news, capital, and business transactions are the main commerce of the new world economy. This kind of global market, Walter Wriston observes, has "fundamentally altered" the power of banks or governments to control events. Whenever anything happens anywhere, "thousands of computer screens light up," and traders buy or sell. "This enormous flow of data has created an Information Standard which has replaced the gold standard and the Bretton Woods agreements," he says. "The electronic global market amounts to a giant vote-counting machine which conducts a running tally of what the world thinks of a government's diplomatic, fiscal and monetary policies." The information standard differs from all its predecessors because no nation can resign from what amounts to a global plebiscite. The result, says Wriston, is that "the very definition of sovereignty is changing."[25]

Another fact that sets the information standard apart

from previous standards is its unique nature. It is based not on anything solid like gold but on speeding electrons that cannot even be seen. The DNA of the new global economy is information; it is the transmitter of technology, the driver of production, and the carrier of social and political change. As W. Michael Blumenthal argues, information is "a basic resource as important today as capital, land and labor have been in the past."[26] Together, the global information industry—including media, telecommunications, computers, and other related systems—was worth $1.3 trillion in 1990 and is projected to reach $3 trillion in 2000—the equivalent of one out of every six dollars of world GNP.[27] Moreover, electronic information differs radically from oil, coal, iron, or any of the other commodities that dominated international relations in the industrial age and even earlier eras. Information is not confined to territory like Dutch East Indian oil, for which Japan waged a war. It is not consumed like wheat; it can be shared by millions or hundreds of millions and never be depleted. It cannot be destroyed; books can be burned but not knowledge. Once new information is transmitted, sold, or stolen, it cannot be repossessed like a car; it is locked in minds beyond the reach of process servers.

All sorts of practical implications flow from these facts. Japan, Taiwan, Singapore, and South Korea, for example, were able to charge to the front lines of world competition not just because of lower labor costs but because the principal raw materials of modern success are information and technology. They could import these without duty and exploit them without cost. Global capital, converted into binary bits and traveling at nearly the speed of light, moves more freely and in larger volumes than conventional trade. National regulations falter. Knowledge also creates new products, new markets, and even runs factories so that global production has become more mobile than people. By the mid-1980s, international production—goods and services produced within a country by foreign companies—had grown larger than international trade, in which the goods and services of one country are sold to another.[28] Information also is more difficult to price or tax or patent, and this produces major regulatory struggles. "The technology of printing came into being in the same era as the nation-state and both seem to be reaching the end of their usefulness in the era of the computer," says Oxford's Anthony Smith. "It is physically impossible to impose upon data the same kinds of controls that are imposed upon goods and paper-borne information, though the world will inevitably continue to try for some years."[29]

Politics cannot operate independently of economics, as demonstrated by the reform movements in the former Soviet Union and also, though less obviously, in China. So the economic repercussions of the information standard are felt also in the politics of nations and in international relations. Deng Xiaoping underlined this himself in 1992 when, at the age of eighty-seven, he traveled to the capitalist-style special economic zones of Shenzhen and Zhuhai to make one of his rare public appearances. "Whoever is opposed to reform must leave office," he warned, signaling the priority of economic development over ideology.[30] But to promote vigorous economic development, a nation must open its borders to massive flows of information, data, and capital. This forces it to surrender many of the controls that have always defined its sovereignty, and, carrying the logic still further, the whole structure of international relations has to be recast. The embattled General Agreement on Tariffs and Trade, for instance, is ill equipped to deal with intangibles like cross-border data transfers and intellectual property. Indeed, the unauthorized passage of electronics through obsolete laws of sovereignty opens the way to a number of classic international conflicts: freedom of information and free trade versus censorship and protectionism. Unrestricted movement of news and entertainment versus cultural autonomy and social regulation. Foreign dominance versus technological independence. And, above all, national autonomy and self-reliance versus national mergers and the submission of sovereign rights to the imperatives of market alliances.

In fact, the submission of sovereignty to market imperatives is already taking place. This can be seen in a major worldwide trend toward the formation of both international business alliances and regional economic blocs. Illustrating the convergence of transnational business interests was a series of collaborative agreements in 1992 in the semiconductor industry. In one of these, IBM in the United States, Toshiba in Japan, and Siemens in West Germany pooled their resources to develop dynamic random access memory chips. In another agreement, Advanced Micro Devices in the United States joined with Japan's Fujitsu to develop flash memory and other chips. Advanced's chairman, W. D. Sanders III, who had been an outspoken critic of Japan, said that "the world has changed and globalization is the future"; apparently, nationality mattered less than before.[31]

Nationality is also being eroded in the rush to form economic blocs based on shared technological and economic interests rather than Cold War fears. More and more, nations are finding they have to merge their affairs with other countries in order to be more competitive economically and, as a corollary, to be more effective politically. Just as colonies once paid in their own sovereignty for the industrial growth of imperial powers, so now must modern nations pay in their sovereignty for global profit. Examples of regionalist trends are the still integrating European Community and the

North American Free Trade Area initiated by the United States and Canada and projected to include Mexico and other regional members. Latin American countries, long more oriented toward Europe than toward one another, have also been scrambling to form free trade zones: the Mercosur group, including Argentina and Brazil; the Andean Pact, which includes Venezuela and Colombia; the Caricom group in the Caribbean and Central America.

In Asia, natural economic territories (NETs) are crisscrossing old political barriers under the pressures of mutual interest. One triad links Guangdong in China to Hong Kong and Taiwan. Another NET combines China's Shandong province with South Korea. The ASEAN nations are busy trying to form an economic alliance in Southeast Asia, where Japan is also establishing a de facto regional economic powerhouse. Walt W. Rostow, among others, sees an emerging "age of regionalism" driven by a "remarkable revolution in communications" and other new technology. The nation-state, he says, simply cannot cope by itself with "the complex economic and technological interdependencies of the contemporary world."[32] For in the affairs of nations, as in business, electronic life puts a premium on larger units.

The immediate motivation for regionalism is economic—the need to operate on a larger scale to compete in a dynamic global system—but an erosion of sovereignty is also involved, and this can force political change and even political unions. In the European Community, for example, national political rights are being subordinated to regional economic necessity. This restricts national autonomy in foreign as well as domestic affairs and, not surprisingly, invites resistance, most notably in the case of Great Britain, with its memories of past imperial glory and centuries-old aloofness from the continent. Prime Minister Margaret Thatcher thunderclapped against any surrender of British sovereignty, and her successor, John Major, protested, though in milder tones. Nevertheless, the community plunged ahead at the end of 1991 with the historic treaty of Maastricht, which called for cutting away more chunks of sovereignty with commitments, for example, to a common currency and to the idea of European citizenship. "Call it what you will," said *The Economist,* "by any other name it is federal government."[33] Waves of popular resistance rolled in against the treaty in 1992, providing Europe's leaders with a jolting reminder of their dependence on public opinion. But the imperatives of a competitive global economic system still worked in favor of regional integration and against sovereign separatism.

It would be a great convenience if trends were all moving in the same direction, but history is not so accommodating. While the global economy is imposing regional togetherness on some nations, ethnic nationalism is tearing others apart. And, potentially even more worrisome, the same surging technology that is propelling the global economy is also creating an ominous gap between advanced industrial nations and developing countries of the Third World. The United States, Japan, members of the European Community, and a few other countries are accumulating and capitalizing on high technology at such an astonishing rate that no one else is even in contention. Not only are many countries failing to catch up but they are falling behind the pace of development. Whole areas of the world remain outside the technology-information loop at a time when some kind of technological parity is absolutely critical to economic progress and, ultimately, to global political stability.

It is true, as we have seen in earlier chapters, that television, VCRs, and global communications have penetrated into the most remote corners of the earth. Cameroon is on the global computer network Internet. Asiasat services and mobile telephone systems are turning up in surprising places. People everywhere are tuned into the world. For the most part, however, they are receivers, not producers, of technology; TV sets and radios may be plentiful, but the computers, the educational base, the technologically savvy work force, and the other infrastructures needed in a high-tech economy are missing. And this injures a nation politically as well as technologically. As Anthony Smith notes in his classic discussion *The Geopolitics of Information,* "a society with no access to satellite sensoring data about itself is unable to control its own economic destiny and can in no real sense any longer be thought to be 'free.' "[34] These problems are particularly evident in much of Africa and in the Arab world, where technical gaps are made even wider by fundamentalists who actively oppose Western ideas. The result is that on the one hand television tells mass audiences how much better their life could be while on the other hand lagging technological development dooms their chances for that life. This exacerbates the disparity between haves and have-nots and prompts charges in UNESCO and elsewhere of a new Western imperialism based on monopolies of knowledge.

Criticism originally was centered on so-called cultural aggression—the flooding of developing countries with Western films and news. Now, however, many areas have indigenously produced movies, videos, and TV programming. India, in fact, is the largest film producer in the world. Iran's thriving film industry has turned out movies that have won international recognition. Also, regional news exchanges like Asiavision, the launching of communications satellites by the Arab League, India, Indonesia, Brazil, Mexico, and other countries, and the growth of independent news outlets in the Third World have chipped away at Western dominance of news.

In a tougher competitive sense, however, the issue is not news and culture so much as the kind of hard information—the constant inflows of technical reports and ideas, the data, and the know-how—that designs products, drives machines, and literally runs huge economies. Educational levels and technical experience define a country's ability to absorb the onrush of technology that it needs to compete. "The capacity of a nation—not just of its government but of society as a whole—to adjust to rapidly changing techno-economic, socio-cultural and political changes," said Soedjatmoko, the late Indonesian authority on development, "very much depends on its collective capacity to generate, to ingest, to reach out for, and to utilize a vast amount of new and relevant information."[35] The high-tech nations have this capacity, but many of the developing nations do not, and the gulf between the two extremes is a geopolitical disaster waiting to happen.

One might expect the foreign policy establishment to take the lead in attacking long-term problems like the North-South gap. But thanks to the communications revolution and new technology, the old world of diplomacy is itself in ruins. During the long ascendancy of realpolitik, international relations were defined, as Raymond Aron once observed, as a game played by diplomats and soldiers on behalf of statesmen. Professionals like George Kennan resembled the scribes of ancient Egypt, so steeped in recondite knowledge that they alone were qualified to preside over the affairs of state. They considered public opinion a vulgarity and had only disdain for politicians, journalists, and, more often than not, the statesmen who employed them. Now, however, every Tom, Dick, and Harry is trampling over their red carpets. They are no longer the chief custodians of policy. Their arts are the arts of an era that has disappeared; their glory, like Miniver Cheevy's, lies in a past that is gone.

The channels of diplomacy that used to run directly from government to government under the jealously guarded management of foreign ministries are now broad freeways of interaction connecting societies at every level of social, economic, technological, and political interest. International relations have grown infinitely larger and more diverse than they were only a few decades ago. More than ever, foreign and domestic policies are mixed in the same pot. Thousands of individuals, corporations, special interest groups, government agencies, and international organizations are all pursuing their own agendas with their foreign counterparts. Both elected officials and ordinary citizens, seeing the world on the tube every night, are beguiled into believing they are more informed than they are. The mystery of foreign affairs is dissipated, the reverence for expertise eroded, and common opinion given more status as a guide to foreign policy.

"When egalitarianism is the prevailing passion," says Kennan, there is a widespread belief that "there is no function of public life that could not best be performed by a random assemblage of gray mediocrity" and that "to admit that some people might be more suitable than others would be an *élitiste* thought—hence inadmissible." The qualities which set the professional diplomat apart from his fellow citizens are "especially odious," he notes glumly, because they can only be acquired outside "those great currents of mass reaction and emotion to which American society is uniquely vulnerable and by which journalists and politicians, above all others, are carried."[36]

To the horror of the professional, diplomacy has become the politician's sport, with heads of government making policy by television and telephone and traveling the planet to be seen personally grappling with the world's crises. They like to commune together, preferably on location in front of cameras, rather than through layers of experts. So foreign affairs—and wars—are run out of presidential offices, with hot line calls, summits galore, and, as the Moscow coup illustrated, instant TV diplomacy on CNN's message network.

While State Department specialists are left somewhere in Foggy Bottom, decisions fall into the hands of White House aides who may be experts on election campaigns but are Humpty Dumptys in international relations. And ambassadors become a threatened species, like snail darter fish. They seldom make the group pictures at summits anymore and even have trouble squeezing into arrival and departure coverage of globe-trotting foreign ministers. Their status has fallen so low that George Ball turned down a choice appointment with the comment: "I did not wish to end my days as an innkeeper for itinerant congressmen."[37] When Jordan's King Hussein saw George Shultz on CNN saying something he objected to, he didn't call his ambassador or foreign minister; he telephoned the network's headquarters in Atlanta to rush his personal reply onto the air. Another time, when he had been criticized for siding with Iraq in the Gulf crisis, he quickly responded with a live CNN interview. In both cases, he considered television the best way to communicate his position directly to President Bush and other key world leaders. A king, raised in the traditions of an earlier time, had come to terms with a somber new fact of international life: the invasion of foreign affairs by public opinion and the media.

"Any discussion of changes in the diplomatic system must begin," says Abba Eban, "with the most potent and far-reaching transformation of all: the collapse of reticence and privacy in negotiation. The intrusion of the media into every phase and level of the negotiation process changes the whole spirit and nature of diplomacy. The modern negotiator cannot escape the duality of his role. He must transact business simultaneously with his negotiating partner and his own public opinion. . . . Whether this is a favorable development or not is irrelevant; it is certainly irreversible."[38]

It is customary to blame the media for this new state of affairs, and it is true that they are often in the thick of things—relaying messages during the democracy uprisings in Beijing, for example, or serving as go-betweens between the Amal militia and Washington at the time of the TWA hostage crisis. When Anwar Sadat made his famous trip to Jerusalem, he left his wife home but took Barbara Walters, Walter Cronkite, and John Chancellor with him. However, really dictating the new media diplomacy are not journalists, even celebrity anchors, but the medium itself. It is communications technology that has changed the relationship between people and government and forced diplomacy onto the world's stages, where every issue and every negotiation is exposed to public scrutiny and political manipulation.

This has transformed international relations, as Eban observes, but not the diplomatic profession itself. Despite the momentous changes taking place around them over the last several decades, all hands in the foreign policy establishment remained tuned to the standard political frequencies: Soviet threats, power balances, and diplomatic maneuvers. They thought in terms of government-to-government relations rather than in the multilayered transactions of an emerging interdependent global system. In the very years when new technology and transnational corporations were laying the foundations for the world economy that now dominates the international scene, the State Department did not have enough state-of-the-art specialists to fill a closet.

"Is there any reason," asks one American diplomat, "why the U.S. embassy in Japan, our biggest economic rival, should have far more political than economic officers?"[39] In a brutally candid report in 1992, the Carnegie Commission on Science, Technology, and Government condemned the State Department and the entire foreign policy community for failing to develop any competence in science and technology at a time when these fields were driving "many of the central issues on the world's agenda." In 1992, the State Department had fewer than thirty science officers covering the world yet remained so resistant to change, according to the commission, that many experts despaired of ever seeing any improvement.[40]

Similarly, while communications technology was making public opinion a major force in international relations, it was mostly ignored by the political specialists who dominate the diplomatic corps, experts in reporting the comings and goings of high officials but confirmed amateurs in the new arts of media politics and opinion manipulation.

The State Department originally considered public opinion so tangential to its mission that it shunted the burden off to the U.S. Information Agency. In 1981, Assistant Secretary of State Kenneth L. Adelman argued that public diplomacy had become critically important because "the masses are the subjects and no longer merely the objects of historic change."[41] Yet he defined this diplomacy so narrowly—as little more than "telling America's story" and selling decisions after they have been made by we-know-best officials—that he clearly did not recognize how his world had changed. Although Henry Kissinger was a master at manipulating media heavyweights, his larger specialty was conspiracy and secrecy. Other secretaries of state thought more in terms of private negotiation than of the uses of public opinion. And the foreign service generally could not see beyond the shadows of its comfortable tradition.

The result, as former ambassador to Iran William H. Sullivan has noted with resignation, was that countries like Israel skillfully "orchestrate the public dimensions of their diplomacy" while American diplomats treat public opinion as an afterthought. "In almost any one of the endless Washington meetings that determine a course of diplomatic action," he said, "the final question . . . as the participants are rising from the table and moving toward the door is 'What do we say to the press about this?' "[42] Totally missing is any sense of the new reality of the electronic age: the absolute centrality of public opinion in international affairs. The fact is that the tracking, analyzing, and mobilizing of public opinion—domestic and foreign—must be the core of policymaking, not an accessory, not something to be passed off with a press release or propaganda broadcast.

What is new about diplomacy in the electronic age is not merely the disruptive intrusion of the media into sensitive negotiations, as Eban mostly defines it, but the corollary need to marshal domestic and foreign public opinion to achieve policy outcomes that conventional diplomacy cannot deliver. More and more, political leaders have to influence foreign publics as well as their fellow statesmen to get things done. President Bush and Prime Minister Thatcher, for example, waged a major publicity campaign to bolster Mikhail Gorbachev's position with his own people. Then Bush and Prime Minister John Major used similar tactics to stiffen support for Boris Yeltsin during his struggle with the Kremlin coup plotters. And in April 1992, the Group of Seven hastily announced a Russian aid program to help Yeltsin fend off critics during a risk-laden meeting of the Congress of People's Deputies.

More important than the size of the program, Andrei Kozyrev, Russia's foreign minister, emphasized, was the timely targeting of aid and the promoting of "coverage in the mass media" to provide a psychological lift for people struggling to learn a new life.[43] With the growth of this kind of media diplomacy, the center of gravity tends to shift from foreign offices to heads of government. And the business of integrating domestic and foreign opinion into the policy-making process falls, partly by default, under the influence of miniature foreign ministries in the offices of presidents, with media consultants and image factories supplying much of the stagecraft.

Some countries have been quicker than others to recognize the opinion factor. Israel is easily the most formidable practitioner in the United States, although it has a special advantage in the support of Jewish American organizations. Japan, by contrast, has virtually no political constituency, yet it is remarkably successful in getting its viewpoints across, even if it doesn't win many friends. As mentioned earlier, it has a whole army of lobbyists, media mercenaries, and former American officials plugging its position in its fractious disputes with the United States. "A Japanese public relations machine," says the well-known Dutch critic Karel Van Wolferen, "effectively amplifies what government agencies and the Keidanren want Americans to believe." A flurry of TV interviews and newspaper articles, for example, trumpeted Japan's contributions to the U.S. economy together with the thesis that American manufacturers have only themselves to blame for their troubles.

By contrast, Van Wolferen observes, "no comparable American effort has gone into swaying Japanese opinion" because U.S. officials believed this could be left to a "reasoned discourse among Japanese themselves."[44] And this, as much as anything else, speaks eloquently to the failure of the foreign policy establishment in Washington to understand the critical need to compete for public opinion in contemporary international affairs. To leave this function to White House image-makers or to the U.S. Information Agency is to ignore an essential new instrument of policy-making and further erode the influence of professional diplomats.

What all these trends mean is that the foundations of the international system are shifting. Increasingly assertive publics undermine the supremacy of ruling elites and enhance the importance of public opinion in foreign affairs. Economics supersedes power politics as the dominant factor in policy-making. Phenomenal increases in the volume and diversity of international transactions overrun traditional patterns of government-to-government relations. Professional diplomats lose control over their old domain. Modern communications riddle frontiers and erode national sovereignty. And while television stimulates consumer desires, frustrations rise dangerously when they cannot be satisfied by countries that have been left in the backwaters of technology.

Everywhere, profound changes come in a rush, too fast for understanding or effective responses. A new age has arrived—or is in the process of arriving—but the institutions that will be needed to organize it have not yet been put in place. International relations are in transition and disarray. This is not so much a fact to be grasped as a state of motion to be felt.

VIII

No Time for Wisdom

ASTRONOMERS, GAZING AT TODAY'S HEAVENS, read the history of the universe in the ancient light of stars. So too can we see in the light of our own time the paths that have led us to where we are. We are the future of our past. Today's condition is the result of earlier causes, and present trends will be the templates of tomorrow's world. The past exists in the present and the present will be part of the future, as T. S. Eliot once suggested.[1] Hidden in all that is happening now are the codes of the future, the infinitely complex interactions of man, nature, and technology that will determine the character of life on earth in the twenty-first century, which is nearly upon us.

If we could unravel the codes of change as genetic engineers decipher the codes of life, we might be able to modify global behavior and affect, if ever so slightly, the unfolding contours of the coming age. But we do not look for causes. In our obsession with a self-centered present, we prefer to deal with the calamities that have already arrived rather than look for those that are about to occur. We specialize in instant emotional response rather than thoughtful anticipation. We live for the existential moment, carpe diem as Horace said, instead of searching for the future. So folly and surprise are our constant condition. And we are trapped again and again in the ambushes of history.

These habits of the human spirit are a liability in any age but especially so now, when global life is changing too fast and too radically to be left safely to the accidents of chance. People power, transnational corporations, mass consumerism, egalitarian demands, ethnic aggressions, mingling and colliding civilizations—a thousand streams of social and economic turbulence—surge through the world at electronic speeds. New sensations and trends rush at us in confusing whirls, shortening the distance from cause to effect, shrinking the time between the first stirrings of discontent deep within a society and the sudden outbursts of protest and violence on the ramparts of politics. Political leaders, preoccupied with the daily illusions of power, do not even hear the hissing fuses before they are knocked down by the explosions. George Bush had no clue to social failure in the United States until he walked among the charred ruins of south-central Los Angeles in 1992, filling TV screens with images of presidential concern but also presenting the world with a model of leadership operating behind the curve of public need.

The unprecedented velocity and scale of change, in large part the work of the communications revolution, mean that new trends have to be caught at much earlier stages if there is to be any chance of altering their course and affecting outcomes; the faster a baseball travels toward the plate, the sooner a batter has to start his swing. It was a "tardy and tortuous" response to the social repercussions of the Industrial Revolution, as Reinhold Niebuhr and Paul E. Sigmund observed, that undermined confidence in liberal democracy and gave Marxism its opening to power.[2] Similarly, the incredible blindness of American institutions to a gathering storm of industrial and social disorder contributed to the great national disaster that followed in the 1930s. Now the human upheavals are incomparably greater, universal in their diversity and global in their embrace, and again the institutions of society respond too slowly and too little.

Popular expectations, stimulated by mass media and market-driven consumerism, soar beyond fulfillment. Aroused masses, awakened at last to their value and power, demand more than governments are prepared to deliver. Promises of democracy that glowed in communist darkness lose their luster in the glare of democratic reality, when people must run a gauntlet of political chaos and personal angst to certify their freedom. The ideals of individualism and egalitarianism are driven to distorting extremes. And nearly everywhere the pursuit of immediate satisfaction— individual, ethnic, or national—takes precedence over communal concern for the future. Consumed with a tumultuous present, the world posts few sentinels to stand watch for tomorrow's dangers.

So, to cite one example, the technological gap between North and South grows ominously larger, away from television's lenses and beyond the West's vision. François Mitterrand once warned that this imbalance could lead to new tragedies, even to another world war by the end of the century.[3] But the problem is almost totally ignored because a striking feature of the new global economy in the electronic age is the narcissism of the principal actors. The great transnational corporations are wheeling and dealing across old national frontiers, in a prevailing spirit of nonregulation, driven by private ambitions unrelated to the long-term policy goals of any country—or their own long-term self-interest, for that matter. They are scratching and clawing, merging and unmerging, scrambling everywhere to defeat competitors and expand market empires. Their emphasis is on free trade when they are trying to penetrate other markets and on protectionism when they are themselves being threatened; few look beyond their own quarterly earnings.

The governments of high-tech nations are infected with the same self-centered altruism. Japan walls off its domestic economy while it invades the United States, swarms over East Asia, and threatens Europeans. Even the European Community, while denying it is building a "fortress Europe," is focusing its entire attention on making itself the largest, most competitive, and least vulnerable market in the world. In the advanced industrialized world, that is, because this is where the main battles are being fought for power and position in the electronic century.

What is missing is any concern for the other side of the human equation—any thought about the impact that all this economic activism is having, and will increasingly have, on developing nations still lingering in the limbos of the Industrial Revolution. As fast as many of these countries are moving, the high-tech countries are moving faster; the technological distance between North and South widens instead of narrows, and the danger of new conflicts and violence grows with it. At a time when the very speed of social change and the rising voices of once silent masses require earlier social detection and more farsighted policy-making, concerns for the future are blindfolded by an all-consuming present.

The great irony is that the forces which are driving the information age also make it more difficult to cope with the social and political repercussions. The mass market capitalism now being installed as a global economic model trumpets the virtues of consumerism, personal fulfillment, and immediate satisfaction. In the process, it devalues the ideals of self-sacrifice and public service, which are critical to the success of any society, especially now, in a time of historic transition. The mass communications revolution meanwhile intensifies human stress by simultaneously accelerating social change and shortening the time for social adjustment. Worse, it floods the human psyche with sensations that raise emotions but smother thought. In the world of media hype and entertainment, life is for today, not tomorrow; there are no rewards for thinking ahead.

Mass communications also lengthen the distance between the mindset of leaders and the reality they must confront. Memories are the ghosts that haunt statesmen; impressions and experiences recalled from earlier years become the instincts that rule them when they are summoned to power. Munich . . . World War II . . . the "loss" of China . . . the Berlin blockade . . . Korea. These were the commanding memories that led America into Vietnam and on to humiliation. After that, Vietnam became the haunting remembrance . . . the fear of another piecemeal defeat in an unexplainable cause . . . the real reason Bush ordered instant military victory rather than slow-acting sanctions in Iraq . . . the explanation for the generals' insistence on overwhelming firepower . . . to heal the wounds of failure. And now, what is the controlling memory? The collapse of communism? A misplaced euphoria about a new world order?

The problem is that the emotional reflexes which statesmen develop during their formative years do not fit the conditions they face when they finally reach high office. And then they are too harassed by daily crisis to absorb new knowledge and shift mental gears. They find it is easier to live with the beliefs they already have, even if these are wrong, than adjust to new ideas, even if they are right. "Mental standstill or stagnation—the maintenance intact by rulers and policymakers of the ideas they started with," said Barbara Tuchman, "is fertile ground for folly."[4] When new ideas come in torrents, as they do now, memories are more quickly outdated; the dichotomy between mindset and challenge becomes more pronounced. So we see the gap between Gorbachev the Communist Party infighter and Gorbachev the reformer, and the struggle between Deng Xiaoping hero of the Long March and Deng Xiaoping champion of China's march to modernity. In a more static time, when great technological and social changes were separated by decades or even centuries, the differences between remembered experience and contemporary problems were not so large. Leaders, standing on steadier social and economic ground, could keep closer company with political reality.

Now, as President Clinton noted in his inaugural address, the sights and sounds of history are broadcast instantaneously to billions around the world. "Communications and commerce are global, investment is mobile, technology is almost magical, and ambition for a better life is now universal," he said. "We earn our livelihood in America today in peaceful competition with people all across the earth. Profound and powerful forces are shaking and remaking our world. And the urgent question of our time is whether we can make change our friend and not our enemy."

But what can be done? It is an article of American faith that no mountain is so high that it cannot be climbed. But the beginning of wisdom is to recognize that for many problems there are no solutions. Or if solutions do exist that they are usually not found until the problems have died of natural causes or been replaced by new and larger ones. In the case of the electronic age, complexity challenges understanding and deep contradictory forces challenge solutions. One is more awed by limitation than by possibility. Yet possibility should be examined. The pursuit of perfection is worthwhile even if the goal is never reached because ideals are the fuel of aspiration and aspiration is the fuel of life.

In many ways, the great challenge of our time is to avoid

the political blindness and tortuous institutional responses that have turned other great turning points of history into seedbeds of social breakdown and war. It is to search out the dangers lurking in today's events in hopes of preventing at least some of tomorrow's disasters. And this means pursuing an ideal—the ideal of prevention. Preventive governance. Preventive diplomacy. Preventive journalism. A systematic and continuing effort to deal with causes before they become results, to attack problems in the deepest recesses of society before they grow into political crises and then uncontrollable explosions.

Politics has always been the endgame in human affairs. It deals with the deeper movements in society only when they have finally risen to the surface and are crises on their way to calamity. Politicians mainly operate in the rear echelons of ideas and change. But this is no longer satisfactory, if it ever was; when trends are moving at nearly the speed of light, an addiction to delay is fatal. Societies are changing too fast, publics are too active, and problems too formidably complex. Even to begin to cope, politics has to become involved in the earliest stages of stress. The preventive process has to begin not with bureaucrats and elites huddled around a crisis that has already appeared on the evening news but with people on the front lines of life, where new crises are being created. Government has to start with sociology, or the science of "non-logical actions" in Vilfredo Pareto's apt phrase.[5] It has to search out the subtle tensions, moods, and trends beneath the surface of society that are the incubators of disaster. Long-simmering problems like low productivity, poor educational performance, sexual harassment, and inner-city failures should not have to blow up before they attract official attention. Social detection needs to replace political surprise, and crisis avoidance needs to be more honored in government than crisis management.

These same principles of prevention apply in foreign affairs. Traditional diplomacy, with its emphasis on political reporting and ministerial relations, almost guarantees that the precursors of crisis will be missed. Listening carefully to the shah of Iran did not provide any clues to the revolution rumbling beyond the Peacock Throne. What is needed, as suggested in the last chapter, is a diplomacy that specializes in the disheveled mass emotions and shifting popular opinions that now play such an important role in decision making. A diplomacy which tracks the social, economic, and technological trends that signal where a country is going instead of where it has been.

The whole axis of international relations has now changed from Cold War politics—balances of military power, ideological competition, and surrogate wars—to economics (with its emphasis on technological progress, market shares, and higher living standards) and social betterment (with its emphasis on personal satisfaction, human rights, and environmental protection). These historic shifts call in turn for a historic change in the orientation and culture of professional diplomacy. Social analysis, public diplomacy, and crisis prevention need to be pursued as much or more than political reporting, negotiation, and crisis management. "Foreign offices are full of experts on diplomatic relations, not interdependence," says Lincoln P. Bloomfield. "Crisis managers take justifiable pride in their capacity for rapid response. But it is the over-the-horizon problems, left unanalyzed and unintegrated into present policies, which guarantee incessant surprises for the 'practical' diplomats." Foreign affairs, he observes, now requires "integrative thinking" that cuts across domestic as well as foreign issues and across old agency rivalries and tribal differences. "Large and small powers alike," Bloomfield says, "need new mental and conceptual tools for their survival in a world essentially beyond their control."[6]

Ideally, journalists should also put more emphasis on preventing disasters and less on reporting them. They, too, should be looking past today's breaking news to discover the hidden pockets of misunderstanding, the undetected human tensions that will burst into the headlines tomorrow, next week, or a month or year from now. It is no longer enough for reporters to provide the videotapes of war, to stand on the sidelines of history, being the chroniclers of reaction, reporting today's catastrophes while another unseen world throbs with warnings we do not hear.

The fact is that many of the most fateful issues facing the world lie beyond the reach of American-style journalism, mainly because it is a system that specializes in action and confrontation rather than in the more subtle forces of change. Whereas it is superb at covering riots, it is ill-equipped to uncover the causes of riots in time for society to avoid them. Yet this has to be one of the critical tests of a journalistic tradition—its ability to probe deeply into the currents of change in its own society and in the world generally so that the public can form timely and accurate judgments for its own protection. The media have flunked this test too often to justify their smug resistance to change.

Immediate action and controversy are the dominant fare at most newspapers, and superficiality bathed in entertainment and fiction is the chief product of television. The media's mission to inform democracy would be better served if they redefined news to emphasize thought as well as action, harmony as well as conflict, explanation as well as exposure. If they were more resistant to the TV staging and manipulation which overly emotionalize news and interfere with rational deliberation. And, most important, if they pursued a new kind of journalism that is preventive rather than merely reactive.

This kind of journalism would search out the causes of social breakdowns before they turn into the failures and violence which the TV shows now celebrate. In the case of foreign news, it would look into societal trends on a sustained, long-term, and global basis. It would mean a huge investment in money, professional interest, and institutional time. And, most challenging of all, it would mean confronting the natural resistance of readers and viewers—citizens and voters who must ultimately decide how well they will be informed but who still find immediate action news more appealing than analytic and prospective reporting that seems remote from their immediate lives. Formidable obstacles, indeed, perhaps insuperable. But an effective international warning system is a life-and-death matter, and journalists as well as political leaders and diplomats have an obligation to provide it if they can.

The final hours of the twentieth century are a rare moment in the human story, when we stand at the edge of time and can actually see history's changing of the guard: one era departing and another taking its place, the dying Industrial Revolution yielding to a new age of high technology and mass information. Whole civilizations shifting like tectonic plates as they are ground together by the pressures of rapid modernization. Mass societies and hundreds of millions of people interacting in an interdependent global economy and emergent world society. Old patterns of life, old views of the world, old certainties torn away. Enormous personal stresses, social fractures, and lagging government responses. The celebration of capitalism's victory muted by rising tensions between the rich and poor, between rival economic empires, between great ethnic and religious systems on the parapets of cultural confrontation.

That we are able to witness so much change in so brief a period can be attributed to the collapsing of time by motion. In making the speed of light absolute, Einstein and Poincaré made time relative. So as modern technology spins the earth more quickly, the velocity of life increases and time contracts. When change moved no faster than an oxcart, the landmarks of civilization were spread out across centuries or even millennia. But when change moves with the speed of a computer, history is compressed into years, months, or days. Like stars in the expanding universe, the past recedes ever more rapidly. Already, Russia's war in Afghanistan, China's Cultural Revolution, and America's Watergate are only vague memories. The lessons of even a few years ago—of the Cold War, for example—now seem stale and irrelevant. Just as the past rushes backward, the present rushes forward. Today's change immediately becomes tomorrow's reality. "The world will change more in the next 10 years than in any other period in history," says the French economist Jacques Attali.[7] This means that to learn from history one must learn from the present, because history now is the present. It is in current change that new cataclysms are germinating. And it is in the communications revolution, the supreme catalyst of change, that many of the codes to the future can be found. Trends it is generating today provide crucial insights into tomorrow's world.

Only insight can produce foresight, and only foresight offers any chance of prevention. Reason argues that the world should this time avoid the social and political blindness that followed World War I and other troubled transitions in history. But this is not a time of reason. Mass information is not the same as knowledge, and sound bites are not the same as wisdom. Folly is still the dominant gene in the human race. One can only hope against hope that civilization will find a peaceful passage to the twenty-first century.

Notes

1: Contagion of Freedom

1. George F. Kennan, interview on *MacNeil/Lehrer NewsHour,* Aug. 22, 1991, quoted by Neil A. Lewis, "Kennan Says Failed Coup Eclipses '17 Revolution," *The New York Times,* Aug. 24, 1991, p. A9.

2. Anatoly Sobchak, "Breakthrough," *Moscow News,* Sept. 1–8, 1991, p. 10.

3. News conference, Aug. 22, 1991.

4. Eduard Shevardnadze, *The Future Belongs to Freedom* (New York: Free Press, 1991), p. 207.

5. Anna Husarska, "The Apartment," *The New Republic,* Sept. 16–23, 1991, p. 14.

6. Tatyana Tolstaya, "When Putsch Comes to Shove," *The New Republic,* Sept. 16–23, 1991, p. 18.

7. The station was also referred to as Radio DC or Radio of the House of Soviets.

8. Vitali Tretiakov, "Appel aux Journalistes Libres du Monde Entier," *Nezavisimaya Gazeta,* Courier International edition, Paris, Aug. 20, 1991, p. 1.

9. Shevardnadze, *The Future Belongs to Freedom,* pp. 206–207.

10. Leonid Gordon, "Let People at Least Scream," *Moscow News,* Oct. 13–20, 1991.

11. Igor Baranovsky, "Bush Couldn't Get Through to Gorbachev," *Moscow News,* Sept. 11, 1991, p. 13.

12. Anatoli S. Chernyayev, "Four Desperate Days," *Time,* Oct. 7, 1991, pp. 28–29. Excerpts from the diary he kept while held captive on Foros with Gorbachev.

13. Andrew Rosenthal, "Bush Looks Ahead to Accelerated Soviet Reforms and Greater Stature for Yeltsin," *The New York Times,* Aug. 22, 1991, p. A15.

14. Baranovsky, "Bush Couldn't Get Through."

15. Interview, Sept. 20, 1991.

16. David Hoffman, "Global Communications Network Was Pivotal in Defeat of Junta," *The Washington Post,* Aug. 23, 1991, p. A27.

17. William H. McNeill. The first quotation is from "The Peasantry's Awakening All Over the World," *The Washington Post,* national weekly edition, Jan. 7–13, 1991, pp. 24–25. The second is from "Winds of Change," in *Sea-Changes: American Foreign Policy in a World Transformed,* Nicholas X. Rizopoulos, ed. (New York: Council on Foreign Relations Press, 1990), p. 189.

18. Daniel Bell, *The Winding Passage* (Cambridge, Mass.: Abt Books, 1980), p. 60.

19. Ellen Mickiewicz, *Split Signals: Television and Politics in the Soviet Union* (New York: Oxford University Press, 1988), p. 179.

20. William H. McNeill, *A World History* (New York: Oxford University Press, 1979), p. 537.

II: THE NEW ANATOMY OF KNOWLEDGE

1. Interview, Feb. 10, 1990.

2. See "Cable Television Revolution," a series of articles in *India Abroad,* March 29, 1991, pp. 20–22; also Edward A. Gargan, "TV Comes In on a Dish, and India Gobbles It Up," *The New York Times,* Oct. 29, 1991.

3. Marshall McLuhan, *Understanding Media: The Extensions of Man* (New York: New American Library, 1964), especially chapters 8 and 9. See also McLuhan's introduction to Harold A. Innis, *The Bias of Communication* (Toronto: University of Toronto Press, 1951), pp. xi and xiii.

4. Elizabeth L. Eisenstein, *The Printing Revolution in Early Modern Europe* (Cambridge: Cambridge University Press, 1983), pp. 41–90.

5. Walter Lippmann, *Public Opinion* (New York: Free Press, 1922), p. 61.

6. McLuhan, *Understanding Media,* pp. 157–158.

7. Samuel Enoch Stumpf, *Socrates to Sartre* (New York: McGraw-Hill, 1966), pp. 280–286. See also George Herbert Mead's elaboration as reported in Melvin L. DeFleur and Sandra Ball-Rokeach, eds., *Theories of Mass Communication* (New York: Longman, 1982), pp. 120–122.

8. McLuhan, *Understanding Media,* p. 87.

9. See McLuhan, *Understanding Media,* and J. Samuel Bois, quoted in *Theories of Mass Communication,* DeFleur and Ball-Rokeach, eds., p. 136.

10. From *An Introduction to Chinese Civilization,* John Meskill, ed. (New York: Columbia University Press, 1973), p. 601.

11. Quoted by Harold A. Innis, *The Bias of Communication* (Toronto: University of Toronto Press, 1951), p. 62.

12. Edwin O. Reischauer, *The Japanese* (Cambridge, Mass.: Harvard University Press, 1977), p. 385.

13. David A. Stockman, *The Triumph of Politics: How the Reagan Revolution Failed* (New York: Harper & Row, 1986), p. 7.

14. Theodore H. White, *America in Search of Itself* (New York: Harper & Row, 1982), p. 182.

15. Quoted by Michael J. O'Neill, *Terrorist Spectaculars: Should TV Coverage Be Curbed?* Twentieth Century Fund Paper (New York: Priority Press, 1986), p. 17.

16. Interviews plus Zantowsky's comments quoted by Benjamin C. Bradlee in *The Washington Post,* national weekly edition, July 23–29, 1990, p. 23, and the secret police account in *International Herald Tribune,* Nov. 28, 1991.

17. Walter Goodman, "The Inherent Bias, Good or Bad, of the Mindless Eye," *The New York Times,* June 7, 1989, p. C17.

18. Daniel Bell, *The Winding Passage* (Cambridge, Mass.: Abt Books, 1980), p. 23.

19. Private communication, Aug. 19, 1992.

20. Gerald Clarke, *Fame Magazine,* Nov. 1988.

21. Edgar Snow, *Red Star over China* (New York: Bantam Books, 1978), pp. 216–217.

22. Colin Cherry, *World Communication: Threat or Promise?* (Chichester: John Wiley, 1978), p. 7.

23. Quoted by David Dubal, *Reflections from the Keyboard: The World of the Concert Pianist* (New York: Summit Books, 1984), pp. 166–167.

24. Jacques Ellul, *The Technological Society* (New York: Alfred A. Knopf, 1965), p. 378.

25. Ibid., p. 379.

26. Stephen Spender, *Eliot* (Glasgow: Fontana Press 1975), p. 161.

III: THE GLOBAL SPREAD OF MASS SOCIETIES

1. Daniel Bell, *The Cultural Contradictions of Capitalism* (New York: Basic Books, 1976), p. 69.

2. Ellen Mickiewicz, *Split Signals: Television and Politics in the Soviet Union* (New York: Oxford University Press, 1988), p. 204.

3. William H. McNeill, "Winds of Change," in *Sea-Changes: American Foreign Policy in a World Transformed*, Nicholas X. Rizopoulous, ed. (New York: Council on Foreign Relations Press, 1990), p. 168.

4. Comments during the symposium "China's New Revolution," John King Fairbank and Joan Shorenstein Barone centers, Harvard University, June 5, 1989.

5. Ibid.

6. W. W. Rostow, *The Stages of Economic Growth*, 2d ed. (London: Cambridge University Press, 1971), pp. 10–11.

7. "America's Decadent Puritans," *The Economist*, July 28, 1990, p. 11.

8. James Chad, "Dreams for Sale," from *Far Eastern Economic Review*, reprinted by *World Press Review*, July 1990, p. 68.

9. Quoted by Edward A. Gargan, "Village Life in India Is Invaded by Big City Tastes," *The New York Times*, April 16, 1992, p. A4.

10. Fujioka Wakao, "Learning to Live the Good Life," *Japan Echo*, Summer 1989, pp. 30–34.

11. "Japan's Consumer Boom: The Pricey Society," *The Economist*, Sept. 9, 1989, pp. 21–24.

12. James Sterngold, "Thrift Is Under Siege in Japan As Use of Credit Cards Soars," *The New York Times*, June 16, 1992, p. A1.

13. Steven R. Weisman, "More Japanese Workers Demanding Shorter Hours and Less Hectic Work," *The New York Times*, Mar. 3, 1992, p. A8.

14. Ford S. Worthy, "A New Mass Market Emerges," *Fortune*, special "Pacific Rim 1990" issue, 1990, pp. 51–55.

15. Bell, *Cultural Contradictions of Capitalism*, pp. 232–236.

16. Gopal Saksena, "TV Advertising in India—Social Implications," *COMBROAD*, Commonwealth Broadcasting System Association, no. 6, Mar. 1990, pp. 7–11.

17. Daniel Bell, *The Winding Passage* (Cambridge, Mass.: Abt Books, 1980), p. 60.

18. Joshua Meyrowitz, *No Sense of Place: The Impact of Electronic Media on Social Behavior* (New York: Oxford University Press, 1985), p. 133.

19. Interview, Sept. 20, 1991.

20. "Does 'Buy American' Mean Buying Trouble?" *The New York Times*, Jan. 27, 1992.

21. Everett M. Ehrlich, "Informational Technology, Global Linkage, and U.S. Competitiveness," address to the International Trade Facilitation Council, June 14, 1989, in *Vital Speeches*, Oct. 1, 1989, pp. 755–759.

22. Robert E. Lipsey, "America's Multinational Corporations: The Untold Success Story," paper for Tocqueville Asset Management Corp., Feb. 1990, pp. 5–6.

23. Much of this data is cited by Robert B. Reich in "Who Is Us?" *Harvard Business Review*, Jan.–Feb. 1990, pp. 53–64.

24. Pekka Tarjanne, secretary general, UN International Telecommunications Union, at *Business Week* conference on "The Future of World Telecommunications and Information Technology," May 2–3, 1990.

25. Susan Strange, "The Name of the Game," in *Sea-Changes*, pp. 238–271.

26. Reich, "Who Is Us?" p. 59.

27. James Fallows, "Containing Japan," *The Atlantic,* May 1989, p. 54.

28. Quoted by Amitai Etzioni, "New Hopes, Old Habits," *The National Interest,* Spring 1990, p. 97.

29. Akio Morita and Shintaro Ishihara, *The Japan That Can Say No* (Tokyo: Kobunsha, 1989), private translation, p. 61.

30. Ibid., p. 16.

31. " 'Joke' Angers A-bomb Survivor but Tokyo Plays It Down," *Los Angeles Times,* Mar. 5, 1992, p. 9A.

32. Address to Chinese military commanders in Beijing, June 9, 1989.

33. Peter Tarnoff, "New Special Relationships," *Foreign Affairs,* Summer 1990, p. 72.

34. Walter Dean Burnham, *The Current Crisis in American Politics* (New York: Oxford University Press, 1982), p. 269.

IV: THE RISE OF PEOPLE POWER

1. Daniel Lerner, "The Revolutionary Elites and World Symbolism," in *Propaganda and Communication in World History,* 2, Harold D. Lasswell, Daniel Lerner, and Hans Speier, eds. (Honolulu: University Press of Hawaii, 1980), p. 387.

2. Makau wa Mutua, director of the Africa Project of the Lawyers Committee for Human Rights, "African Renaissance," *The New York Times,* May 11, 1991, p. 23.

3. From Arnold J. Toynbee, *A Study of History,* abridged (New York: Oxford University Press, 1947), p. 278.

4. Alexis de Tocqueville, *Democracy in America* (Garden City, N.Y.: Anchor Books, 1969), p. 435.

5. Walter Lippmann, *Public Opinion* (New York: Free Press, 1922), pp. 125, 54.

6. Ibid., p. 132.

7. Tocqueville, *Democracy in America*, p. 435.

8. Franco Ferrarotti, *The End of Conversation* (London: Greenwood Press, 1988), p. 52.

9. Alan B. Durning, "Worldwatch Paper 88," Worldwatch Institute, Jan. 1989, p. 8.

10. *Democracy in Developing Countries: Africa*, Larry Diamond, Juan J. Linz, and Seymour Martin Lipset, eds. (Boulder, Col.: Lynne Rienner Publishers, 1988), p. 26.

11. *Democracy in Developing Countries: Asia*, Larry Diamond, Juan J. Linz, and Seymour Martin Lipset, eds. (Boulder, Col.: Lynne Rienner Publishers, 1988), pp. 25–26.

12. Sheryl WuDunn, "Slow-Motion Revolution Reshapes China," *New York Times Service*, International Herald Tribune, Sept. 19, 1991.

13. Quoted by Bernard Weinraub, "Some in India Grieve for Their Country, Too," *The New York Times*, June 6, 1991, p. 3A.

14. Ariel Dorfman, *Bread and Burnt Rice*, quoted in Durning, "Worldwatch Paper 88," p. 21.

15. Interview, Feb. 26, 1990.

16. Interview, Mar. 22, 1990.

17. Interview, Henrikas Yushkiavitshus, vice chairman of Gosteleradio, Mar. 17, 1990; he is now UNESCO's assistant secretary general for public information.

18. S. Frederick Starr, "Soviet Union: A Civil Society," *Foreign Policy*, Spring 1988, pp. 32–41.

19. Ellen Mickiewicz, *Split Signals: Television and Politics in the Soviet Union* (New York: Oxford University Press, 1988), pp. 4–5, 179.

20. Gail W. Lapidus, "State and Society: Toward the Emergence of Civil Society in the Soviet Union," in *Inside Gorbachev's Russia*, Seweryn Bialer, ed. (Boulder, Col.: Westview Press, 1989), p. 129.

21. S. Frederick Starr, "A Usable Past," *The New Republic*, May 15, 1989, p. 27.

22. Gleb Pavlovsky and Maxim Meyer, "Public Movements in the USSR," quoted in *Moscow News*, Feb. 25–Mar. 4, 1990, p. 89.

23. "Worldwatch Paper 88," p. 13.

24. Lapidus, "State and Society," p. 129.

25. S. Frederick Starr, "New Communications Technologies and Civil Society," in *Science and the Soviet Social Order*, Loren R. Graham, ed. (Cambridge, Mass.: Harvard University Press, 1980), p. 43.

26. Jonathan C. Randal, "Popular Discontent Hits French-Speaking Africa," *The Washington Post*, Mar. 26, 1990, p. A17.

27. *Newsweek*, May 19, 1989.

28. Casualty figures used in the trial of Coman, see "Eight Ex-Romanian Officials Get Jail for Slayings in Timosoara," *The New York Times*, Dec. 10, 1991, p. A5.

29. Timothy Garton Ash, *The Magic Lantern* (New York: Random House, 1990), p. 94.

30. Ibid., pp. 141–142.

31. Stan Sesser, "A Reporter at Large: A Rich Country Gone Wrong," *The New Yorker*, Oct. 9, 1989, pp. 55–96.

32. Edmund S. Morgan, *Inventing the People: The Rise of Popular Sovereignty in England and America* (New York: W. W. Norton, 1988), pp. 38, 39.

33. For this discussion, see *Democracy in Developing Countries: Latin America*, Larry Diamond, Juan J. Linz, and Seymour Martin Lipset, eds. (Boulder, Col.: Lynne Rienner Publishers, 1988), pp. 35–37.

34. *Democracy in Developing Countries: Africa*, p. 26.

35. Robert A. Scalapino, "The United States and Asia: Future Prospects," *Foreign Affairs*, Winter 1991–92, p. 25. See also his "Asia and the United States: The Challenges Ahead," *Foreign Affairs*, 1989–90, pp. 89–90.

36. Lucian W. Pye, "Communication, Development, and Power," in *Propaganda and Communication in World History*, 2, Harold D. Lasswell, Daniel Lerner, and Hans Speier, eds. (Honolulu: University Press of Hawaii, 1980), p. 439.

37. Scalapino, "The United States and Asia," p. 91.

v: Central Casting for Leaders

1. Bernard Weinraub, "Mondale Farewell," *The New York Times*, Nov. 8, 1984, p. A1.

2. James MacGregor Burns, *The Power to Lead* (New York: Simon & Schuster, 1974), p. 43.

3. Henry Kissinger, private comment to author, Apr. 15, 1985.

4. Hedrick Smith, *The Power Game* (New York: Random House, 1988), p. 398.

5. Robert E. Denton, Jr., *The Primetime Presidency of Ronald Reagan* (New York: Praeger, 1988), p. 3.

6. Leo Braudy, *The Frenzy of Renown* (New York: Oxford University Press, 1986), p. 551.

7. Quoted in Richard Nixon, *Leaders* (New York: Simon & Schuster, 1990), p. 56.

8. Ibid., p. 56.

9. Jack W. Germond and Jules Witcover, *Whose Broad Stripes and Bright Stars?* (New York: Warner Books, 1989), p. 54.

10. Denton, *Primetime Presidency,* p. 66.

11. Arthur M. Schlesinger, Jr., *The Cycles of American History* (Boston: Houghton Mifflin, 1986), p. 293.

12. Interview, Dr. Svetlana G. Kolesnik, assistant research professor, Moscow University, Mar. 19, 1990.

13. *Folha de São Paulo,* cited in "TV Making Obscure Brazilian the Candidate to Beat at 39," *The New York Times,* July 16, 1989.

14. "Brazil: Film Finance in the Age of Hyperinflation," *Sight and Sound,* Spring 1990.

15. Quoted in E. J. Dionne, "Fiction Mirrors Loss of Majesty," *The New York Times,* April 17, 1989, p. B10.

16. Franco Ferrarotti, *The End of Conversation* (London: Greenwood Press, 1988), p. 72.

17. Personal communication to author, Aug. 19, 1992.

18. Maureen Dowd, "Bush Ventures Little and Gets Along Fine," *The New York Times,* Sec. 4, Jul. 23, 1989, pp. 1 and 4.

19. Michael Cockerell, *Live from Number 10* (London: Faber & Faber, 1988), p. xiii.

20. Ibid., pp. 213–217.

21. Ibid., p. 253.

22. Quoted in Julian Barnes, "Letter from London," *The New Yorker,* Mar. 5, 1990, p. 95.

23. Tony Schwartz, "The Prime Minister and the Media," in *min, Media Industry Newsletter,* Mar. 27, 1991.

24. This material was drawn partially from reporting by Joachim Holtz in *Die Zeit* of Hamburg, reprinted in *World Press Review,* Sept. 1986.

25. "Talk of the Town," *The New Yorker,* July 9, 1990, pp. 25–26.

26. Schlesinger, *Cycles of American History,* p. 269.

vi: Crisis of Governance

1. Kevin P. Phillips, *Mediacracy: American Parties and Politics in the Communications Age* (Garden City, N.Y.: Doubleday, 1975), p. ix.

2. Mary Collins, "News of the Congress, by the Congress," *Washington Journalism Review,* June 1990, p. 32.

3. From a fine summary analysis by Michael Oreskes, "American Politics Loses Way as Polls Displace Leadership," *The New York Times,* Mar. 18, 1990, p. A1.

4. *MacNeil/Lehrer NewsHour,* Apr. 10, 1992.

5. Pat Choate, "Political Advantage; Japan's Campaign for America," *Harvard Business Review,* Sept.–Oct. 1990, p. 87.

6. Randall Rothenberg, "The Journalist as Maytag Repairman," *Gannett Center Journal,* Spring 1990, p. 108.

7. Jill Smolowe, "Paranoia Run Amuck," *Time,* Sept. 30, 1991, p. 44.

8. Rochelle L. Stanfield, "Lobbyists for the Lowly," *National Journal,* Aug. 4, 1990, p. 1882.

9. *Chicago Tribune,* Dec. 25, 1991.

10. *MacNeil/Lehrer NewsHour,* Apr. 10, 1992.

11. Peter F. Drucker, *The New Realities* (New York: Harper & Row, 1989), pp. 99–100.

12. Maureen Dowd, "White House Concocted Drug Buy for Speech," *The New York Times,* Sept. 23, 1989, p. A1.

13. Michael K. Deaver with Mickey Herskowitz, *Behind the Scenes* (New York: William Morrow, 1987), p. 141.

14. Quoted in *Campaign for President: The Managers Look at '88,* David R. Runkel, ed. (Dover, Mass.: Auburn House, 1989), p. 136.

15. Hedrick Smith, *The Power Game* (New York: Random House, 1988), pp. 412–413.

16. Bill Kovach, "Shaping the News," *Nieman Reports,* Spring 1991, p. 2.

17. Don Bolz, "In Medias Res: If You Can't Beam 'Em, Bypass 'Em," *The Washington Post* national weekly edition, May 25–31, 1992, p. 12.

18. James MacGregor Burns, *The Power to Lead* (New York: Simon & Schuster, 1984), p. 159.

19. Lloyd N. Cutler, "Foreign Policy on Deadline," *Foreign Policy,* Fall 1984, p. 117.

20. Abraham F. Lowenthal, "Rediscovering Latin America," *Foreign Affairs,* Fall 1990, p. 33.

21. I. M. Destler, Leslie H. Gelb, and Anthony Lake, *Our Own Worst Enemy: The Unmaking of American Foreign Policy* (New York: Simon & Schuster, 1984), p. 151.

22. Cutler, "Foreign Policy on Deadline," p. 121.

23. "Ted Turner's CNN Gains Global Influence and 'Diplomatic' Role," *The Wall Street Journal,* Feb. 1, 1990, pp. A1, A6.

24. George H. Quester, *The International Politics of Television* (Lexington, Mass.: Lexington Books, 1990), p. 166.

25. Interview by my researcher Elizabeth Malkin, Jan. 15, 1991.

26. For this comment and other related campaign tactics, see Miriam Horn, "Campaign Carnival," *The New Republic,* July 2, 1990.

27. Harold Evans, former editor of *The Sunday Times* and *The Times* of London, Grenada Guildhall Lecture, 1974.

28. Interview, Sept. 19, 1991.

29. Alexander Merkushev, "The Russian and Soviet Press: A Long Journey from Suppression to Freedom via Suppression and Glasnost," Joan Shorenstein Barone Center, Harvard University, Aug. 1991.

30. "Asiavision As an Example of Regional TV News Exchanges in the South," presented at the Fourth International Broadcast Workshop, Málaga, Apr. 12–16, 1986 (Friedrich Ebert Stiftung, 1987).

31. *Nieman Reports*, Winter 2, 1990, p. 8.

VII: New World Disorder

1. Andrew Rosenthal, "Blurred Image," *The New York Times*, Apr. 21, 1991, Sec. 4, p. 1.

2. Evan Thomas and Ann McDaniel, "Where Was George This Time?" *Newsweek*, Apr. 15, 1991, p. 31.

3. Strobe Talbott, "When Monsters Stay Home," *Time*, Apr. 15, 1991, p. 30.

4. "Sanctuary for the Kurds," *The Economist*, Apr. 20, 1991, p. 12.

5. United Nations Population Fund report, Apr. 29, 1992.

6. Daniel Bell, "Some Simple Predictions about Planet Earth in 2013," *The Washington Post*, national weekly edition, Feb. 22–28, 1988, p. 25.

7. Abba Eban, *The New Diplomacy: International Affairs in the Modern Age* (New York: Random House, 1983), p. 10.

8. Timothy J. McNulty, "Decisions at the Speed of Satellite," *Chicago Tribune*, Dec. 22, 1991, pp. A1, A18.

9. Arno A. Penzias, "Futures in System Integration" (paper presented in Dallas), Jan. 24, 1991.

10. Eban, *New Diplomacy*, p. xiii.

11. The comment in 1777 of the French writer Le Trosne, quoted in Eban, p. 331.

12. Stanley Hoffmann, "A New World and Its Troubles," in *Sea-Changes: American Foreign Policy in a World Transformed*, Nicholas X. Rizopoulos, ed. (New York: Council on Foreign Relations Press, 1990), p. 280.

13. Susan Strange, "The Name of the Game," in *Sea-Changes*, p. 241.

14. Andrew Arno, "The News Media as Third Parties in National and International Conflict," in *The News Media in National and International Conflicts*, Andrew Arno and Wimal Dessanayake, eds. (Boulder, Col.: Westview Press, 1984), pp. 237–238.

15. "Europe Protests," *The Economist*, June 24, 1989, pp. 11–12.

16. William B. Wood, George J. Demko, and Phyllis Mofson, "Ecopolitics in the Global Greenhouse," *Environment*, Sept. 1989, pp. 14–15.

17. Robert A. Dahl, *Democracy and Its Critics* (New Haven, Conn.: Yale University Press, 1989), pp. 219–220.

18. I am aware that Kirkpatrick's argument was more nuanced, making a distinction between rights violations in communist countries, which she said never evolve into democracies, and authoritarian but noncommunist regimes that do. As it turned out, however, some communist regimes did evolve in a democratic direction, and the rights movement was a salutary factor in the change.

19. Christoph Royen, member of Research Council, Stiftung Wissenschaft and Politik, Ebenhausen, interview, Mar. 5, 1990.

20. Quoted in Donald Wilhelm, *Global Communications and Political Power* (New Brunswick, N.J.: Transaction Publishers, 1990), p. 117.

21. "Observing Nicaragua's Elections, 1989–1990," Council of Freely Elected Heads of Government, Special Report No. 1, Carter Center, Emory University, p. 12.

22. Stanley Hoffmann, "Reaching for the Most Difficult: Human Rights as a Foreign Policy Goal," *Daedalus,* Fall 1983, p. 33.

23. Craig Whitney, "Sign of World Transformed: A Rights Meeting in Moscow," *The New York Times,* Sept. 10, 1991, p. A15.

24. Quoted in Eban, *New Diplomacy,* p. 145.

25. Walter Wriston, remarks for International Institute of Communications, Sept. 13, 1988. Also see his brilliant book, *The Twilight of Sovereignly: How the Information Revolution Is Transforming our World* (New York: Charles Scribner's Sons, 1992), *Passim*.

26. W. Michael Blumenthal, "Technological Change," *Foreign Affairs,* 1987–88, Vol. 66, No. 3, p. 534.

27. *The Economist,* Feb. 29, 1992, p. 17.

28. For a discussion of this phenomenon see Strange, "Name of the Game," p. 242.

29. Anthony Smith, *The Geopolitics of Information* (New York: Oxford University Press, 1980), p. 131.

30. Quoted in *Wen Wei Po* and cited in *The New York Times,* Feb. 10, 1992.

31. *The New York Times,* July 16, 1992.

32. W. W. Rostow, "The Coming Age of Regionalism," *Encounter,* June 1990, pp. 3–7.

33. "Europe's Dutch treat," *The Economist,* Dec. 14, 1991, p. 13.

34. Smith, *Geopolitics of Information,* p. 114.

35. Soedjatmoko, quoted by Edward Ploman, in *InterMedia*, Sept. 1981, p. 11. See also Soedjatmoko's *The Primacy of Freedom in Development*, Anne Elizabeth Murase, ed. (Lanham, Md.: University Press of America, 1984).

36. Kennan does not recall where he originally made these comments but does not doubt they are genuine.

37. George W. Ball, *The Past Has Another Pattern* (New York: W. W. Norton, 1982), p. 452.

38. Eban, *New Diplomacy*, p. 345.

39. From "Too at Home Abroad," by a Foreign Service officer writing under a pseudonym in *The Washington Monthly*, Sept. 1991, p. 18.

40. "Science and Technology in U.S. International Affairs," Carnegie Commission on Science, Technology, and Government, Jan. 1992.

41. Kenneth L. Adelman, "Speaking of America: Public Diplomacy in Our Time," *Foreign Affairs*, Spring 1981, p. 915.

42. William H. Sullivan, "The Transformation of Diplomacy," Fletcher Forum, Summer 1981, p. 293.

43. Andrei Kozyrev, "Russia: A Chance for Survival," *Foreign Affairs*, Spring 1992, p. 9.

44. Karel Van Wolferen, "The Japan Problem Revisited," *Foreign Affairs*, Fall 1990, p. 51.

VIII: No Time for Wisdom

1. See T. S. Eliot's "Burnt Norton," *The Complete Poems and Plays, 1909–1950* (New York: Harcourt, Brace & World, 1971), p. 117.

2. Reinhold Niebuhr and Paul E. Sigmund, *The Democratic Experience* (New York: Praeger, 1969), p. 28.

3. Interview with James Reston, *The New York Times,* June 4, 1981.

4. Barbara W. Tuchman, *The March of Folly* (New York: Alfred A. Knopf, 1984), p. 383.

5. Lewis A. Coser, *Masters of Sociological Thought,* 2d ed. (New York: Harcourt, Brace & World, 1971), p. 388.

6. Lincoln P. Bloomfield, *The Foreign Policy Process: A Modern Primer* (Englewood Cliffs, N.J.: Prentice-Hall, 1982), p. 185.

7. Jacques Attali, *Millennium: Winners and Losers in the Coming World Order* (New York: Times Books, 1991), p. 120.

Index

MICHAEL J. O'NEILL is a former editor of the New York *Daily News* and a past president of the American Society of Newspaper Editors. He is the author of several books, including *Terrorist Spectaculars: Should TV Coverage Be Curbed?* and *China Today.* He lectures widely in the United States and abroad. A member of the Council on Foreign Relations and the National Committee on United States–China Relations, he is also a former vice chairman of the Japan Society. O'Neill spent most of his early career as a Washington correspondent for United Press and then the *Daily News,* mainly covering international affairs. He has written for a wide variety of publications, including *Newsweek, The New York Times,* and *The Wall Street Journal.*